The Grand Tour of William Beckford

William Beckford was born in 1760, the only child of an extremely wealthy family. His father was a sugar tycoon in the West Indies and his mother was a granddaughter of the sixth Earl of Abercorn. A much cherished child, William Beckford never went to school. He was reputedly taught piano by Mozart and drawing by the painter Alexander Cozens. He went on the Grand Tour with his tutor at the age of twenty and was encouraged to keep notes on his travels. His later career included the publication of the immensely successful *Vathek* and a homosexual scandal which caused him to withdraw from society, first to Fonthill, where he built a famous gothic folly, and later to Bath. These events led to rumours and then legends of his growing eccentricity.

Elizabeth Mavor has written several novels (one of which was shortlisted for the Booker Prize), a biography of the Duchess of Kingston and *The Ladies of Llangollen* (published by Penguin), which is the Ladies' own story. She is married to the Illustrator Haro Hodson, has two sons and lives in Oxfordshire. Her most recent book, *Life with the Ladies of Llangollen*, is also published in Penguin under the title *A Year With the Ladies of Llangollen*.

WILLIAM BECKFORD

*

· THE GRAND TOUR OF ·
· WILLIAM BECKFORD ·

*

Selections from
Dreams, Waking Thoughts and Incidents

Compiled and Edited by
Elizabeth Mavor

PENGUIN BOOKS

Penguin Books Ltd, Harmondsworth, Middlesex, England
Viking Penguin Inc., 40 West 23rd Street, New York, New York 10010, U.S.A.
Penguin Books Australia Ltd, Ringwood, Victoria, Australia
Penguin Books Canada Limited, 2801 John Street, Markham, Ontario, Canada L3R 1B4
Penguin Books (N.Z.) Ltd, 182–190 Wairau Road, Auckland 10, New Zealand

Published in Penguin Books 1986

Made and printed in Great Britain by
Richard Clay (The Chaucer Press) Ltd,
Bungay, Suffolk
Filmset in Monophoto Ehrhardt

· CONTENTS ·

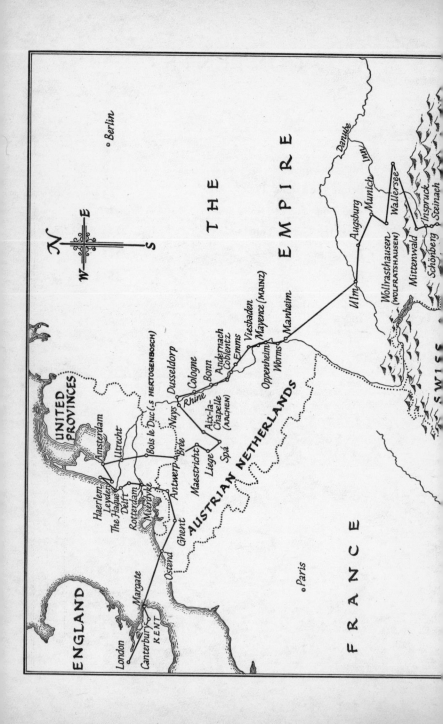

THE GRAND TOUR OF
William Beckford

· INTRODUCTION ·

THE TRAVEL JOURNAL

The Grand Tour of Europe which this Journal celebrates was once considered a high moment in a young man's life. It was not only a justification for the many tedious hours spent learning his *qui quae quod*, but also a journey back in time to the very springs of his culture, to those ruined fragments of an antique world so long held in veneration by Englishmen.

It was a journey that was also thrilling in its own right. Long before Beckford, men had found themselves pleasantly appalled by the pointed horrors of the Alps that intervened between them and the blue skies and landscapes of Italy. 'Precipices, mountains, torrents, wolves, rumblings, Salvator Rosa . . .'[1] commented Horace Walpole in a hushed voice. A few days later he was to describe what happened to his spaniel, Tory,

the prettiest, fattest, dearest creature! I had let it out of the chaise for the air, and it was waddling along close to the head of the horses, on the top of the highest Alps, by the side of a wood of firs. There darted out a young wolf, seized poor dear Tory by the throat, and, before we could possibly prevent it, sprung up the side of the rock and carried him off.[2]

Expectations of the journey through the Alps, and of the curiosities of the southern cities they were to visit, had been wrought up in the minds of prospective travellers long before any Tour was undertaken, by the accounts of those who had preceded them, and by the prints and paintings brought back from the other side. The country they were to visit was thus exotic yet profoundly familiar. 'Now we began to distinguish Murano,' writes Beckford of his first visit to Venice, 'St Michele, St Giorgio in Alga, and several other islands, detached from the grand cluster, which I hailed as old acquaintance;

innumerable prints and drawings having long since made their shapes familiar.'[3]

There was also the pleasing cachet attached to making the Grand Tour, the reputation to be won as a virtuoso, a connoisseur, a Man of Taste in the arts and scenery of the Latin world. There were, of course, pretensions:

> *In curious paintings I'm exceeding nice,*
> *And know their several beauties by their Price.*
> *Auctions and Sales I constantly attend,*
> *But chuse my pictures by a skilful Friend.*
> *Originals and copies much the same,*
> *The picture's value is the painter's name.*[4]

There were also understandable *longueurs*. 'If those who have no taste for the fine arts would fairly own it,' wrote James Boswell, 'it would be better. Mr Damer and Captain Howe, two trueborn Englishmen, were in the great gallery at Florence. They submitted quietly to be shewn a few of the pictures. But seeing the gallery so immensely long, their impatience burst forth, and they tried for a bett who should hop first to the end of it!'[5] This seems not to have been unusual. Somewhat earlier Lady Hertford had written from Florence that 'most of our travelling youth neither improve themselves, nor credit their country,'[6] and, like most Florentine residents nowadays, she dreaded the approach of July, when the city was rendered hideous with tourists.

Beckford, however, was not of this cast. Well grounded in the classics by his tutor, Mr Lettice, with a natural sensibility towards all the arts and with a great love of the natural world, he was surely one of the few Lady Hertford could consider *ought* to have been sent abroad. It would be, moreover, through him, and people like him, that, via music, painting and gardening, the transmuting power of the south would enter English social life.

This selection from the account of his Grand Tour in 1780 is taken from one of the five surviving copies from a total imprint of 500. This text is taken from George Clarke's copy in the Bodleian Library.

Beckford burnt the rest. The account itself has not been widely available in this country for almost sixty years.

Of the original pocket-books upon which the final book of the Tour was based, only one remains. This runs from the 26th to the 31st of October 1780, and is a thin flexible booklet about six inches by four, with a cover marbled pink, grey, slate and yellow, eminently suitable for carrying in the pocket and whipping out for 'on the spot' impressions. This was certainly Beckford's way of working, 'While I stand and write waters bubble around me and I scent the furze in blossom,'[7] he writes in a pencilled fragment from an earlier journal kept when he was making a tour of the English Lakes in 1779.

The one remaining Grand Tour pocket-book is interesting in that it shows the brief notes from which he worked up the final version. 'Left Florence,' he writes on the 26th of October, 'a sober Autumnal Eve: Thunderstorm – Ruins of Castles in the Vale shaded by poplars with faded yellow leaves. Think where I was this time year happy and sequestered with my loved Wm. Night drawing on – arrive at Sienna.'[8]

Many of the longer entries, however, were to go into the published book unaltered, this applying in particular to the extraordinary reverie experienced when he first visited St Peter's in Rome.

The projected book of the Tour must have been rapidly put together, especially when one takes into account the quite immoderate social life Beckford was leading on his return from the continent in April 1781. Most of the entries were edited before the year was out, though a further seven were added the following year while staying at Posillipo with Sir William Hamilton. 'I am exceedingly impatient to look over my Italian Journey and will do my best to make it worth looking at . . .' he had written his tutor, Mr Lettice. 'You know I have set my heart upon the success of my book and shall not at all relish its being only praised as a lively, picturesque excursion . . .'[9]

Of lively picturesque excursions there were at the time a growing number. Thomas Gray, avidly read by Beckford, had powerfully evoked the delightfully horrid charms of both the Grande Chartreuse and, nearer home, Gordale Scar, while lesser-known tourists, like the Reverend Mr Whalley from Bath, pensively meandering through

Savoy with flowers in his hat, were already expatiating upon the cascades, smoking cottages, monks and contented peasants that a new aesthetic was teaching them to find interesting.

Beckford himself was well aware of this trend, was indeed a little caught up in it himself, but he brought to his observations both an original way of looking and an ecstatic energy which were to give his writing exceptional interest.

Such energy enabled him, while staying in Geneva in 1777, to remain a whole day on the summit of Mont Salève, across the French border, minutely tracing in words the wonderfully subtle movements of light and mist, the changing colours and the delicate play of the winds, not to mention the more mundane doings of a peasant and a flock of goats 'staring at me with all their eyes and all their horns'. 'Five hours elapsed,' he finally recorded in a paean reminiscent of Wordsworth. 'Hours of wonder and gratitude. I have been steeped in those sensations which arise from the contemplation of the great objects of nature.' [10]

For such contemplation he had a possibly unique cast of mind. This he had already analysed by the time he was eighteen, '. . . my Reason and my fancy is continually employed, when abandoned by one I obey the other. These two powers are my Sun and Moon. The first dispels vapours and clears up the face of things, the other throws over all Nature a dim Haze and may be styled the Queen of Delusions . . .' [11]

This curious polarity placed him on the frontier between the serene classical landscape, and the mysterious country of the romantics, combining the objectivity of the one, and the evocative and imaginative power of the other.

His imagination had been ignited early on by the reading of oriental tales, and in particular the *Arabian Nights*. His earliest extant story is set in China and Japan, and shows that by fourteen he was already competent in the genre. By the time he was ready to set out on the Grand Tour he was an accomplished writer who had already discovered the form in which he could best express himself – the reverie cast as a letter. 'Think how we should exult at finding ourselves in arched Chambers glowing with yellow Light,' he had written to

Alexander Cozens, his drawing master, 'amidst Vases formed in another Hemisphere and cabalistic Mirrors wherein Futurity is unveiled,'[12] a style of writing that he was later to employ to describe his 'aesthetico/mystico' experience in St Peter's.

Yet imaginative as he was, Beckford could also write with the chaste simplicity of Dorothy Wordsworth, who, rather than Beckford himself, could have been standing by the osier beds that then surrounded the Arch of Constantine to glimpse 'A little cart . . . driving for why or wherefore I know not through the reeds which divided with a low murmur to give it passage. Two peasants plodded after it.'[13] At Coniston Water a year before his mood had been more Keatsean as he gazed at '. . . savage rocky cliffs of a brown uncommon hue that look as if they produced potent herbs such as one may reep by moonlight with a bronze sickle'.[14]

The Europe Beckford was to visit and record was the Europe of the *ancien régime*, and it is perhaps chastening to learn from him how generally well governed, prosperous and content so much of it then was. It is unexpected, moreover, to discover how excellent were the roads over the Alps, how hospitable the peasants, how ubiquitous (as now) what Beckford terms 'the German whisker', and how in 1780 they were already dancing the waltz in Bavaria, 'turning round and round, with a rapidity that is quite inconceivable to an English dancer . . .'[15]

If we learn much about the goings on in that Europe, and of its very great beauty expressed in word pictures as limpid as a painting by Claude or as savage as a mighty set piece by Salvator, or dreamlike as a Turner, we also, rattling along, learn something of Beckford. We find that he is a fanatical non-smoker, a conservationist, an avid sightseer who yet detests the official guides. We catch him casting himself down to dream in flowery grass, then suddenly jumping up and chasing along the mountain-ridges with the wild goats, swinging like a squirrel in a treetop, filling his carriage with jasmine and pulling down the green blinds. He is charming, touchy, funny, infuriating, but never dull.

In this selection it has been painful to leave anything out at all, for once one falls for Beckford's way one tends to want to read everything he wrote. In the event I have confined my selection to the Grand Tour of 1780, leaving out Beckford's account of an earlier visit to the Grande Chartreuse, together with seven further letters that he wrote en route for Naples in 1782. I have also omitted the strangely pompous *Reflections on the Economy, Politics and Fine Arts of Several European Nations*, which rounds off his Grand Tour, and exhibits a chauvinism quite out of character. 'I may justly affirm,' he concludes, no doubt with an eye to placating the 'grown-ups', 'that in commerce, arts and arms, not one of them stands superior to Great Britain!' [16]

For the rest I have clipped some of his more imaginative exuberances, some too of his enthusiastic excesses concerning architecture and the other arts. I only hope that I have not significantly tampered with his essential power of charming the reader, whether by enabling us to see the ordinary transformed, or by evoking so freshly the moment, or by simply making us laugh, so ensuring that whatever else happens, we shall enjoy ourselves.

Garsington
April 1985

·BEFORE THE GRAND TOUR·

He was born on Michaelmas day 1760. A month before, the twenty-three-year-old George III had come to the throne to initiate an era which was to number among its many excitements Watt's steam engine, Dr Johnson, the loss of the American colonies, the phantom holy pregnancy of Joanna Southcott, the paintings of Gainsborough and William Beckford of Fonthill.

He opened his eyes in Alderman Beckford's town house at the corner of Greek Street and Soho Square. Alderman Beckford, a middle-aged sugar tycoon with a rasping Colonial accent, uncouth manners and a boisterous clutch of bastards, was a prominent Cit. Mrs Beckford, the Alderman's wife, had been the widow of another, but she could boast blue blood, for her paternal grandfather had been an Earl. She was also a committed Evangelical.

At the christening of the only legitimate heir to the largest sugar fortune ever made, Lord Effingham stood proxy-godfather for the elder Pitt. 'I consider it the highest honour to have such a sponser to my child,' wrote the Alderman to the great statesman, 'No endeavour of mine shall be wanting,' he added, 'to instil into his tender mind the principles . . . such as you would approve of.' [1]

The instilling began at once in preparation for the young heir's brilliant future. French and his mother tongue were learnt simultaneously, Latin begun at six. It is said that the eight-year-old Mozart came to Fonthill and gravely coached young Beckford in five-finger exercises on the pianoforte. But Beckford also amused himself. He roamed the grounds and explored the richly exotic rooms of his father's fabulous country house in Wiltshire, so aptly named Fonthill Splendens, and when scarcely breeched got into the Alderman's library and there found, and devoured, volumes of oriental tales, in particular the *Arabian Nights*, which was to influence the whole course of his life.

In temperament he took after both parents. When not much more than a baby he exhibited symptoms of the Beckford business acumen by paying deliberate and drawn-out attentions to 'a parcel of cats' doted upon by an old and extremely rich relative. His infant circumspection was ultimately rewarded with an ancient and beautiful *tazza* of brilliants which he ever after referred to as 'the cat diamonds'. He also took after his mother ('the Begum', as he later chose to call her) honouring her own preoccupation with social status by flying into a passion when a friend was so ill-advised as to remind him that one of his great-grandfathers had been a shoemaker. There is no doubt that school would have been good for him – he said as much himself – but it had already been decided to educate him in lonely grandeur at home.

When he was seven Mr Drysdale arrived from Scotland to tutor him. He found his young pupil agreeable, but already beginning 'to think of being master of a great fortune. I am apprehensive,' continued Mr Drysdale, 'that both his mother and father, contrary to their own desires and inclination, may hurt him by indulgence.'[2]

Two years later the Alderman died, leaving his nine-year-old son to a Begum becoming every day more Evangelical, and in the guardianship of an impressive trio of public men: Lord Chatham, Lord Camden and Lord Lyttelton.

The second stage of his education was now set in motion. Mr Drysdale was exchanged for the Rev. John Lettice – 'a good sort of half stupid man,' according to Fanny Burney – who at once commenced the regime approved by Lord Chatham, currently drilling his own young son for eventual political stardom. It was a regime that lasted until Beckford was twenty. Latin, Greek grammar and a chapter of the Bible were ingested before breakfast, after which more lessons took place until one, when Beckford and Mr Lettice went for a ride until dinner at three. Work was then resumed for another hour and a half with light reading before tea, when he chatted with the Begum and her friends or walked in the park. Supper was at nine followed by music or singing until bedtime at eleven.

Happily, when Beckford was about thirteen, room was also found within this rigorous timetable for lessons in architecture (these from

Sir William Chambers who later designed Somerset House) and, more importantly for Beckford, drawing lessons from the artist, Alexander Cozens, who had taught at Eton and now ran a Drawing Academy at Bath.

Cozens was to be the inspiration of Beckford's adolescence. He was a mysterious figure, self-rumoured to be the natural son of Peter the Great by a Deptford barmaid. He had travelled extensively, was an Orientalist and much interested in the occult. Enervated by arithmetic, glazed by too much classical grammar, Beckford turned to him with relief. It was not long before the boy became so preoccupied by Persian, Arabic and Indian lore that the Begum and Mr Lettice grew restive, and with the backing of Lord Chatham the thirteen-year-old was compelled to burn his much treasured collection of oriental drawings. 'Mr Beckford had firmness enough to burn them with his own hand,' reported Mr Lettice with satisfaction to Lord Chatham. 'I hope that as his judgement grows maturer, it will give me an opportunity of acquainting your Lordship with other sacrifices to the same power.'[3]

In fact Beckford was only giving the appearance of conformity. In private he continued to read the forbidden books with avidity, to open his true heart to Cozens, who sympathized with, and shared, his exotic tastes.

'Could I have imagined any person so penetrated with the same rays as you are with those that transfix me?' he wrote. 'Strange, very strange, that such perfect conformity should subsist. All your letters were deposited in a drawer lined with blue, the colour of the Æther.'[4]

From about seventeen onwards, the ambiguous Cozens was Beckford's mentor and confidant, accomplice in his guerilla warfare with the Begum and Mr Lettice. Cozens encouraged his early efforts at writing, shared his jokes: 'State of Fonthill, 1779,' writes Beckford. 'The ladies are pretty sentimental and dawdling. As for the men, I shall say nothing, but that I think them qualified to act the parts of Noodle, Doodle and Foodle in *Tom Thumb* to admiration. Surrounded by such an assembly, my situation (tho' not in Paradise) is as solitary as that of our first Parent when animals alone encircled him.'[5]

His solitude encouraged him to dream, led him to become withdrawn and secretive. Growing concerned the Begum and Mr Lettice put their heads together and determined that it was now time for their protégé to broaden his horizons. He should travel. Geneva, where the Begum had cousins, was fixed upon and in the summer of 1777, when almost seventeen, Beckford and Mr Lettice set out to stay with the Hamiltons. It was not exactly a holiday. Rigorous tuition continued, was expanded to include law, philosophy, physics. Italian was mastered, Spanish and Portuguese begun, but on the side Beckford found the time to devour romances – Ariosto, Tasso, Petrarch, Dante and, more worrying, had the Begum known, he also glutted himself on the gentle melancholy of Thomas Gray's poetry, and Goethe's fashionably tragic *The Sorrows of Young Werther*. To everyone's surprise he began to be sociable, making himself agreeable 'in a way scarcely to be believed', 'doing the agreeable to the ladies in a manner singularly polite and gentlemanly', though nothing could prevent him laughing at two nuns with 'at least 150 quarterings between them', and a plump Baron whose ample waistcoat could have contained seven or eight striplings like himself. He relished enormously the ancient and gloomy castles that he visited. 'Could you transport yourself here in a moment,' he wrote Cozens of one of them, 'you would find me writing in a Bedchamber thirty feet square, hung with old Hobgoblin Tapestry full of Savages and monsters slaughtering one another, which cruelty occasions innumerable streams of red silk to flow copiously from every quarter. If murder were catching we should take care not to lie in this room.'[6] He started a novel dedicated to Cozens. He wandered alone in the mountains. He fell rapturously in love, bewitched by a boy who

seemed to hang on my words, whose eyes drank eager draughts of pleasure from my sight, whose inmost soul was dissolved in tenderness when by chance he touched me, whose countenance was flushed with conscious blushes, who feared to own the passion that stole into every vein and poisoned the serenity of his mind. How he lingered at parting from me, how he departed and returned, confused and not daring to confess for why ... but pined in solitude and consumed his hours in vain lamentations.[7]

It was almost certainly an innocent infatuation, but back at Splendens, the Begum sensing unsuitable vibrations through the ether, set out for Geneva, disliked what she saw, and removed her son that November. On arriving at Dover Beckford wrote to his half-sister that he had

arrived last night in a tottering condition after a most tedious passage of twelve hours during which you may reasonably conjecture our time was pretty well employed. I was fortunately able to own myself the idlest person on board and lay dozing and gaping in the Cabbin whilst everybody else was contributing as much as lay in their power to the Sea. Your Mother bore the voyage admirably well. She is now as well as ever I saw her in my Life.[8]

On their return the Begum began to groom her son for his important entry into fashionable society. He was attractive, slim and well-knit, with blue eyes set over an aquiline nose. Beckford himself remained mutinous. 'I am determined to enjoy my dreams, my phantasies and all my singularity, however irksome and discordant to the worldlings around me,' he wrote in a letter to Cozens. 'In spite of them I will be happy . . .'[9]

His way of being happy was as he said not to 'glory in horses, to know how to knock up and how to cure them, to smell of the stable, swear, talk bawdy, eat roast beef, drink . . .'[10] but rather to take his skiff and row silently upriver between fleets of aquatic birds. 'Surely they *know* it is all my care to protect their peaceful reign,' he wrote, 'to defend them from molestation.'[11] He also chose to play the pianoforte, sing Italian arias and read. These activities further alarmed the Begum. By the following June (1779) and with the object of arousing an admiration for the wholesome, the manly and the patriotic in her difficult son, she organized for him and Mr Lettice a tour of England and its great houses. It was at one of these (something the poor Begum had not foreseen) that he was to meet his terrible destiny. 'What will be my life?' he had asked shortly before. 'What misfortunes wait for me? What glory?'[12]

They set off westwards, taking in on their way a visit to distant cousins at Powderham Castle near Exeter. There were thirteen children in the family, all girls save the youngest, William Courtenay, a clever and pretty boy of eleven, and with his namesake Beckford became instantly infatuated. He described his feelings in what was not so much a letter as a reverie:

It is a sad thing that I cannot see you every day and every hour – since you are the only person (yes let me repeat it once more) to whom I can communicate my feelings – or to whom I can disclose the strange wayward passion which throbs this very instant in my bosom.

His mood now shifted to the self-mocking.

All those who surround me – view me pale – faultering – dejected – desponding – they know not why! What is the matter with you – cries my Mother – tell me for Heavens sake what oppresses you? Have you not every circumstance, every means of happiness in your power – tell me what I can procure for your amusement – I shall instantly command a glittering equipage – shall I invite company – or will you accept the numerous invitations which lie scattered upon your table . . .

Then, evoking an experience well known to some, he began more tellingly:

Great power – who created us both how rapid was the progress of our affection! Surely we must have been inseparable friends in some other existence. We must have doubtless shared the happiness and misery of some other world – or else why did we experience this sudden love for each other . . .[13]

Unsurprisingly, the Begum once more scented danger, and, ever resourceful, but with an inappropriateness that was to mark so many of her dealings with her unfathomable son, she imported Louisa Beckford to assist.

Louisa was the wife of Beckford's first cousin, Peter, a dedicated classicist and fox-hunter, twenty years older than his young wife. He was given to filling his house with sportsmen whom Louisa, bored, delicate and given over to the fashionable cult of sensibility, naturally detested. She and Beckford soon found themselves with much in common, even a fascination with the occult. Beckford gorged upon Louisa's readily available sympathy, she, five years older than Beckford, began to fall in love. By January 1780 he was writing how impatiently he had been waiting to hear from her. 'I have none to awaken me,' he complained, 'none to sympathize with my feelings. Those I love are absent. Thus desolate and abandoned I seek refuge in aerial conversations and talk with spirits whose voices are murmuring in the gales.'[14]

It was silly enough stuff, but it may have prompted the Begum to strike again. It was time to divert her son with new landscapes. Accompanied as ever by the reliable Lettice, he was to set out on The Grand Tour.

They were due to leave in June 1780. On the 16th of April Beckford wrote to Cozens on the subject still uppermost in his mind – William Courtenay:

I have seen him tho' it was but for an hour, and have now but too full an idea of the swiftness of happy moments . . . Judge how I felt upon his telling me that his head had run on nothing but me since we parted, that Fonthill had ever been in his dreams, and that when he crossed Salisbury Plain every distant wood or thicket seemed to belong to it . . . But all my miseries are renewed when I consider how seldom I am doomed to be with him, how little his father or mother comprehend the nature of my love. Who can enter into its refinements, who feel its ardour, who conceive its extent? I mourn single and solitary, without one friend but you to whom I can disclose my melancholy sensations . . .'[15]

It was with such preoccupations that the twenty-year-old Beckford, a pile of small pocket-books beside him in which to record impressions, set off with Mr Lettice on his Grand Tour.

The impressions, written in the form of letters, were addressed to his drawing-master, Alexander Cozens, that ideal correspondent to whom the young writer could communicate his innermost self . . .

· THE TOUR ·

... All through Kent did I dose as usual ... the sun sat before I recovered my senses enough to discover plainly the variegated slopes near Canterbury, waving with slender birch-trees, and gilt with a profusion of broom ... The moment after I got out of the carriage, brought me to the cathedral: an old haunt of mine. I had always venerated its lofty pillars, dim ailes, and mysterious arches. Last night they were more solemn than ever, and echoed no other sound than my steps. I strayed about the choir and chapels, till they grew so dark and dismal, that I was half inclined to be frightened; looked over my shoulder; thought of spectres that have an awkward trick of syllabling men's names in dreary places; and fancied a sepulchral voice exclaiming: 'Worship my toe at Ghent, my ribs at Florence; my skull at Bologna, Sienna, and Rome. Beware how you neglect this order; for my bones, as well as my spirit, have the miraculous property of being here, there, and everywhere.' These injunctions, you may suppose, were received in a becoming manner, and noted all down in my pocket-book by inspiration (for I could not see) and, hurrying into the open air, I whirled away in the dark to Margate ... the first object in this world that presented itself, was a vast expanse of sea, just visible by the gleamings of the moon, bathed in watery clouds; a chill air ruffled the waves. I went to shiver a few melancholy moments on the shore. How often did I try to wish away the reality of my separation from those I love, and attempt to persuade myself it was but a dream!

It was to turn out more of a nightmare, as he wrote Cozens the following day, with 'ten blubbering babes' under his windows and 'a whole legion of fresh imported harlots trumpetting in the other room'.[1]

This morning I found myself more chearfully disposed, by the queer Dutch faces with short pipes and ginger-bread complexions, that came smirking and scraping to get us on board their respective vessels; but, as I had a ship engaged for me before, their invitations were all in vain. The wind blows fair; and, should it continue of the same mind a few hours longer, we shall have no cause to complain of our passage. Adieu! Think of me sometimes. If you write immediately, I shall receive your letter at the Hague.

It is a bright sunny evening: the sea reflects a thousand glorious colours, and, in a minute or two, I shall be gliding on its surface.

Not gliding; the crossing was extremely rough, and they landed 'in a piteous condition' [2] *which may have been responsible for Beckford's jaundiced view of Ostend.*

Ostend, June 21

... I am landed in Flanders, smoked with tobacco, and half poisoned with garlic. Were I to remain ten days at Ostend, I should scarcely have one delightful vision; 'tis so unclassic a place! Nothing but preposterous Flemish roofs disgust your eyes when you cast them upwards: swaggering Dutchmen and mungrel barbers are the first objects they meet with below. I should esteem myself in luck, were the woes of this sea-port confined only to two senses; but, alas; the apartment above my head proves a squalling brattery; and the sounds which proceed from it are so loud and frequent, that a person might think himself in limbo without any extravagance ... You must know then, since I am resolved to grumble, that, tired with my passage, I went to the Capuchin church, a large solemn building, in search of silence and solitude; but here again I was disappointed: half a dozen squeaking fiddles fugued and flourished away in the galleries, as many paralytic monks gabbled before the altars, whilst a whole posse of devotees, wrapped in long white hoods and flannels, were sweltering on either side. Such piety in warm weather was no very fragrant circumstance; so I sought the open air again as fast as I was able. The serenity of the evening, joined to the desire I had of casting another glance over the ocean, tempted me to the ramparts ... but it happened, that I had scarcely begun my apostrophe, before out flaunted a whole rank of officers, with ladies and abbés, and puppy dogs, singing, and flirting, and making such a hubbub, that I had not one peaceful moment to observe the bright tints of the western horizon, or enjoy the series of antique ideas with which a calm sun-set never fails to inspire me. Finding therefore no quiet abroad, I returned to my inn, and should have gone immediately to bed, in hopes of relapsing again into the bosom of dreams and delusions, but the limbo, I mentioned before, grew so very outrageous, that I was obliged to postpone my rest till sugar-plumbs and nursery eloquence had hushed it to repose. At length peace was restored, and about eleven o'clock I fell into a slumber ... Next morning, awakened by the sun-beams, I arose quite refreshed ... No other ideas but such as Trinacria [Sicily] and Naples suggested, haunted me whilst travelling to Ghent. I neither heard the vile Flemish dialect which was talking around me, nor noticed the formal avenues and marshy country which we passed. When we stopped to change horses, I closed my eyes upon the whole scene, and was transported immediately to some Grecian solitude, where Theocritus and his shepherds were filling the air with melody. To one so far gone in poetic antiquity, Ghent is not the most likely place to recall his attention; and, I know nothing more about it, than that it is a large, ill-paved, dismal-looking city, with a decent proportion of convents and chapels, stuffed with monuments, brazen gates, and glittering marbles ... I resolved to journey along with quiet and content for my companions. These two comfortable deities have, I believe, taken Flanders under their especial protection; every step one advances discovering some new proof of their influence. The neatness of the houses, and the universal cleanliness of the villages, shew plainly that their inhabitants live in ease and good-humour. All is still and peaceful in these fertile lowlands: the eye meets nothing but round unmeaning faces at every door, and harmless stupidity smiling at every window. The beasts are as placid as their masters, graze on without any disturbance; and I don't recollect to have heard one grunting swine, or snarling mastiff, during my whole progress. Before every town is a wealthy dunghill, not at all offensive, because but seldom disturbed; and there they bask in the sun, and wallow at their ease, till the hour of death and bacon arrives, when capacious paunches await them. If I may judge from the healthy looks and reposed complexions of the Flemings, they have every reason to expect a peaceful tomb.

But it is high time to leave our swinish moralities behind us and jog on towards Antwerp. More rich pastures, more ample fields of grain, more flourishing willows! – A boundless plain before this city, dotted with cows and flowers, from whence its spires and quaint roofs are seen to advantage! The pale colours of the sky, and a few gleams of watery sunshine, gave a true Flemish cast to the scenery, and every thing appeared so consistent, that I had not a shadow of pretence to think myself asleep. After crossing a broad, noble river, edged on one side by beds of oziers, beautifully green, and on the other by gates and turrets, preposterously ugly, we came through several streets of lofty houses to our inn ... It was almost dusk when we arrived, and, as I am very partial to seeing new objects by this dubious, visionary light, I went immediately a rambling. Not a sound disturbed my meditations: there were no groups of squabbling children or talkative old women. The whole town seemed retired into their inmost chambers; and I kept winding and turning about, from street to street, and from alley to alley, without meeting a single inhabitant. Now and then, indeed, one or two women in long cloaks and mantles glided about at a distance; but their dress was so shroud-like, and their whole appearance so ghostly, I was more than half afraid to accost them. As the night approached, the ranges of buildings grew more and more dim, and the silence which reigned amongst them more aweful. The canals, which in some places intersect the streets, were likewise in perfect solitude, and there was just light sufficient for me to observe on the still waters the reflexion of the structures above them. Except two or three tapers glimmering through the casements, no one circumstance indicated human existence. I might, without being thought very romantic, have imagined myself in the city of petrified people, which Arabian fabulists are so fond of describing ... Reflecting, in this manner, upon the silence of the place, contrasted with the important bustle which formerly rendered it so famous, I insensibly drew near to the cathedral, and found myself, before I was aware, under its stupendous tower. It is difficult to conceive an object more solemn or imposing than this edifice, at the hour I first beheld it. Dark shades hindered my examining the lower galleries or windows; their elaborate carved work was invisible: nothing but huge masses of building met my sight, and the tower, shooting up four hundred and sixty-six feet into the air, received an additional importance from the gloom which prevailed below. The sky being perfectly clear, several stars twinkled through the mosaic of the spire, and added not a little to its enchanted effect. I longed to ascend it that instant, to stretch myself out upon its very summit, and calculate, from so sublime an elevation, the influence of the planets. Whilst I was indulging my astrological reveries, a ponderous bell struck ten, and such a peal of chimes succeeded, as shook the whole edifice, notwithstanding its bulk, and drove me away in a hurry ... Were I not still fatigued with my heavy progress through sands and quagmires, I should descant a little longer upon the blessings of so quiet a metropolis: but it is growing late, and I must retire to enjoy it.

Antwerp, June 23
My windows look full upon the Place de Mer, and the sun, beaming through their white curtain awoke me from a dream of Arabian happiness ... I think it rather selfish to wish you here; for what pleasure could pacing from one dull church to another, afford a person of your turn? I don't believe you would catch a taste for blubbering Magdalens and coarse Madonnas, by lolling in Rubens' chair; nor do I believe a view of the Ostades and Snyders,* so liberally scattered in every collection would greatly improve your pencil. After breakfast this morning, I began my pilgrimage to all those illustrious cabinets [or collections]. First I went to Monsieur Van Lencren's, who possesses a suite of apartments, lined, from the base to the cornice, with the rarest productions of the Flemish School.

Heavens forbid I should enter into a detail of their niceties! I might as well count the dew-drops upon any of Van Huysem's flower-

* Adrian (1610–85) and Isaac Ostade (1621–49), Dutch brothers, painters of low life. Frans Snyders (1579–1657), Dutch still-life and animal painter.

pieces, or the pimples on their possessor's countenance . . . In my way home, I looked into another cabinet, the greatest ornament of which was a most sublime thistle by Snyders, of the heroic size, and so faithfully imitated, that I dare say no ass could see it unmoved. At length, it was lawful to return home; and, as I positively refused visiting any more cabinets in the afternoon, I sent for the harpsichord of Rucker, and played myself quite out of the Netherlands. It was late before I finished my musical excursion, and I took advantage of this dusky moment to revisit the cathedral. A flight of starlings was fluttering about the pinnacle of the tower; their faint chirpings were the only sounds that broke the stillness of the air. Not a human form appeared at any of the windows around; no footsteps were audible in the opening before the grand entrance; and, during the half hour I spent walking to and fro beneath the spire, one solitary Franciscan was the only creature that accosted me. From him I learnt, that a grand service was to be performed next day, in honour of Saint John the Baptist, and the best music in Flanders would be called forth upon the occasion. As I had seen cabinets enough to form some slight judgement of Flemish painting, I determined to stay one day longer at Antwerp, to hear a little how its inhabitants were disposed to harmony . . .

Monday, June 26
We are again upon the pavé [cobbles], rattling and jumbling along, between clipped hedges and blighted avenues. The plagues of Egypt have been renewed, one might almost imagine, in this country, by the appearance of the oak trees: not a leaf have the insects spared. After having had the displeasure of seeing no other objects, for several hours, but these blasted rows, the scene changed to vast tracts of level country, buried in sand, and smothered with heath; the particular character of which I had but too good an opportunity of intimately knowing, as a tortoise might have kept pace with us, without being once out of breath. Towards evening, we entered the dominions of the United Provinces, and had all the glory of canals, trackshuyts, and windmills, before us. The minute neatness of the villages, their red roofs, and the lively green of the willows which shade them

corresponded with the ideas I had formed of Chinese prospects; a resemblance, which was not diminished, upon viewing, on every side, the level scenery of enamelled meadows, with stripes of clear water across them, and innumerable barges gliding busily along. Nothing could be finer than the weather; it improved each moment, as if propitious to my exotic fancies; and, at sun-set, not one single cloud obscured the horizon. Several storks were parading by the waterside amongst flags and osiers; and, as far as the eye could reach, large herds of beautifully spotted cattle were enjoying the plenty of their pastures. I was perfectly in the environs of Canton, or Ning-Po, till we reached Meerdyke. You know fumigations are the current recipe in romance to break the enchantment: as soon, therefore, as I left my carriage, and entered my inn, the clouds of tobacco, which filled every one of its apartments, dispersed my Chinese imaginations, and reduced me in an instant to Holland. Why should I enlarge upon my adventures at Meerdyke? 'tis but a very scurvy topic. To tell you, that its inhabitants are the most uncouth bipeds in the universe, would be nothing very new, or entertaining; so, let me at once pass over the village, leave Rotterdam, and even Delft, that great parent of pottery, and transport you with a wave of my pen to the Hague.

As the evening was rather warm, I immediately walked out to enjoy the shade of the long avenue which leads to Scheveling. It was fresh and pleasant enough . . . I proceeded to the village on the sea-coast, which terminates the perspective. Almost every cottage door being open to catch the air, I had an opportunity of looking into their neat apartments. Tables, shelves, earthen-ware, all glisten with cleanliness: the country people were drinking tea after the fatigues of the day, and talking over its bargains and contrivances. I left them, to walk on the beach; and was so charmed with the vast azure expanse of the ocean which opened suddenly upon me, that I remained there a full half hour. More than two hundred vessels of different sizes were in sight, the last sun-beams purpling their sails, and casting a path of innumerable brilliants athwart the waves. What would I not have given to follow this shining track! . . . All the way home, I reflected upon the œconomical disposition of the Dutch, who raise gardens from heaps of sand, and cities out of the bosom of the waters. I had still further proof of this thrifty turn, since the first object I met, was an unwieldy fellow, (not able, or unwilling, perhaps, to afford horses) airing his carcase in a one-dog chair! The poor animal puffed and panted; Mynheer smoked, and gaped around him with the most blessed indifference!

Beckford was beginning to wilt. 'The heavy air of the Netherlands weighs me down, and I find it is in vain to struggle against the pressure . . .' he wrote to Cozens three days later, on the 29th of June. '. . . O Genius of ancient Greece,' he went on, 'what a horror is this Hague, what lazy canals, what muddy-souled inhabitants! Yesterday I had the misfortune of dining with half a dozen Butterburgs *at Sir J. Yorke's.* There was a total stagnation of wit and genius, but the currency of Roast Beef, Ham and collops of every species made ample amends according to Dutch Ideas – Not a word more can I commit to paper at present. My imagination sinks ten degrees in an instant, how low it will fall, the Damon alone knows, who conducted my steps into this slough of Despond.'* [3]

June 30

I dedicated the morning to the Prince of Orange's cabinet of paintings, and curiosities both natural and artificial. Amongst the pictures which amused me most, is a St Anthony by Hell-fire Brughel;† who has shown himself right worthy of the title; for a more diabolical variety of imps never entered the human imagination. Brughel has made his saint take refuge in a ditch filled with harpies, and creeping things innumerable, whose malice, one should think, would have lost Job himself the reputation of patience. Castles of steel and fiery turrets glare on every side, from whence issue a band of junior devils; these seem highly entertained with pinking poor St Anthony, and whispering, I warrant ye, filthy tales in his ear. Nothing can be more rueful than the patient's countenance; more forlorn than his beard; more

---

* Sir Joseph Yorke (1724–92), Ambassador to the Hague.
† Pieter Breughel the younger (*c.* 1564–1637). Flemish painter, known as 'Hell' or 'Hell-fire' Breughel because he painted scenes with demons and other supernatural beings.

pious than his eye, which forms a strong contrast to the pert winks and insidious glances of his persecutors; some of whom, I need not mention, are evidently of the female kind. But, really, I am quite ashamed of having detained you, in such bad company, so long . . . I went to dine at Sir Joseph Yorke's, with all nations and languages. The Hague is the place in the world for a motley assembly; and, in some humours, I think such the most agreeable. After coffee, I strayed to the great wood; which, considering that it almost touches the town with its boughs, is wonderfully forest-like. Not a branch being ever permitted to be lopped, the oaks and beeches retain their natural luxuriances, and form some of the most picturesque groups conceivable. In some places, their straight boles rise sixty feet, without a bough; in others, they are bent fantastically over the alleys; which turn and wind about, just as a painter could desire. I followed them with eagerness and curiosity; sometimes deviating from my path amongst tufts of fern and herbage. In these cool retreats, I could not believe myself near canals and wind-mills: the Dutch formalities were all forgotton, whilst contemplating the broad masses of foliage above, and the wild flowers and grasses below. Several hares and rabbits passed me as I sat; and the birds were chirping their evening song. Their preservation does credit to the police of the country, which is so exact and well regulated, as to suffer no outrage within the precincts of this extensive wood, the depth and thickness of which, seem calculated to favour half the sins of the capital . . .

Haerlem, July 1st

The sky was clear and blue when we left the Hague, and we travelled along a shady road for about an hour, then down sunk the carriage into a sand-bed; and I, availing myself of the peaceful rate we dragged at, fell into a profound repose. How long it lasted is not material; but when I awoke, we were rumbling through Leyden. There is no need to write a syllable in honour of this illustrious city: its praises have already been sung and said by fifty professors, who have declaimed in its university, and smoked in its gardens; so let us get out of it as fast as we can, and breathe the cool air of the wood near Haerlem; where we arrived just as day declined. Hay was making in the fields, and perfumed the country far and wide, with its reviving fragrance. I promised myself a pleasant walk in the groves, took up Gesner,* and began to have pretty pastoral ideas; but when I approached the nymphs that were disposed on the meads, and saw faces that would have dishonoured a flounder, and heard accents that would have confounded a hog, all my dislike to the walking fish of the Low Countries returned. I let fall the garlands I had wreathed for the shepherds; we jumped into the carriage, and were driven off to the town. Every avenue to it swarmed with people, whose bustle and agitation seemed to announce that something extraordinary was going forwards. Upon enquiry, I found it was the great fair-time at Haerlem; and, before we had advanced much further, our carriage was surrounded with idlers and ginger-bread eaters of all denominations. Passing the gate we came to a cluster of little illuminated booths beneath a grove, glittering with toys and looking-glasses. It was not without difficulty that we reached our inn; and then, the plague was to procure chambers: at last we were accommodated, and the first moment I could call my own has been dedicated to you. You won't be surprized at the nonsense I have written, since I tell you the scene of riot and uproar from whence it bears date. At this very moment, the confused murmur of voices and music stops all regular proceedings: old women and children tattling; apes, bears and shew-boxes under the windows; the devil to pay in the inn; French rattling, English swearing, outrageous Italians, frisking minstrels; *tambours de basque* at every corner; myself distracted; a confounded squabble of cooks and haranguing German courtiers just arrived, their masters following open mouthed; nothing to eat, the steam of ham and flesh-pots all the while provoking their appetite; Mynheers very busy with the realities, and smoking as deliberately, as if in a solitary lust-huys over the laziest canal in the Netherlands; squeaking chambermaids in the galleries above, and prudish dames below, half inclined to receive the golden solicitations of certain beauties for admittance; but positively refusing them, the moment some credible personage appears: eleven o'clock strikes; half the lights in the fair are extinguished;

* Salomon Gessner (1730–88) Swiss writer of sensibility, author of 'The Death of Abel', a prose poem.

scruples grow less and less delicate; mammon prevails, darkness and complaisance succeed. Good night: may you sleep better than I shall!

Utrecht, July 2d

Well, thank Heaven! Amsterdam is behind us: how I got thither signifies not one farthing; 'twas all along a canal, as usual. The weather was hot enough to broil an inhabitant of Bengal, and the odours, exhaling from every quarter, sufficiently powerful to regale the nose of a Hottentot. Under these agreeable circumstances, we entered the great city. The Stad-huys being the only cool place it contained, I repaired thither, as fast as the heat permitted, and walked in a lofty marble hall magnificently covered, till the dinner was ready at the inn. That dispatched we set off for Utrecht. Both sides of the way are lined with the country houses and gardens of opulent citizens, as fine as gilt statues and clipped hedges can make them. Their number is quite astonishing: from Amsterdam to Utrecht, full thirty miles, we beheld no other objects than endless avenues, and stiff parterres,* scrawled and flourished in patterns, like the embroidery of an old maid's work-bag. Notwithstanding this formal taste, I could not help admiring the neatness and arrangement of every inclosure, enlivened by a profusion of flowers, and decked with arbours, beneath which, a vast number of round, unmeaning faces were solacing themselves, after the heat of the day. Each lust-huys we passed, contained some comfortable party, dozing over their pipes, or angling in the muddy fishponds below. Scarce an avenue but swarmed with female josses; little squat pug-dogs waddling at their sides, the attributes, I suppose, of these fair divinities – But let us leave them to loiter thus amiably in their Ælysian groves, and arrive at Utrecht; which, as nothing very remarkable claimed my attention, I hastily quitted, to visit a Moravian establishment at Siest, in its neighbourhood. The chapel, a large house late the habitation of Count Zinzendorf,† and a range of apartments filled with the holy fraternity, are totally wrapped in dark groves, overgrown with weeds, amongst which some damsels

* Formal gravel walks and flower beds.

† Nicolaus Ludwig, Graf von Zinzendorf (1700–60), German religious leader, reformer of the Moravians and founder of the Herrnhut religious community.

were struggling, under the immediate protection of their pious brethren. Traversing the woods, we found ourselves in a large court built round with brick edifices, the grass plats in a deplorable way, and one ragged goat, their only inhabitant, on a little expiatory scheme, perhaps, for the failings of the fraternity. I left this poor animal to ruminate in solitude, and followed my guide into a series of shops furnished with gew-gaws and trinkets, said to be manufactured by the female part of the society. Much cannot be boasted of their handy-works: I expressed a wish to see some of these industrious fair ones; but, upon receiving no answer, found this was a subject *of which there was no discourse*. Consoling myself as well as I was able, I put myself under the guidance of another slovenly disciple, who shewed me the way to the chapel, and harangued, very pathetically, upon celestial love. In my way thither, I caught the distant glimpse of some pretty sempstresses, warbling melodious hymns, as they sat needling and thimbling at their windows above. I had a great inclination to have approached this busy group, but a roll of the brother's eye corrected me. Reflecting upon my unworthiness, I retired from the consecrated buildings, and was driven back to Utrecht, not a little amused with my expedition. If you are as well disposed to be pleased as I was, I shall esteem myself very lucky, and not repent sending you so incorrect a narrative. I really have not time to look it over, and am growing so drowsy, that you will I hope, pardon all its errors, when you consider that my pen writes in its sleep.

Spá, July 6th

From Utrecht to Bois le Duc nothing but sand and heath; no inspiration, no whispering foliage, not even a grasshopper, to put one in mind of Eclogues and Theocritus.* – 'But, why did you not fall into one of your beloved slumbers, and dream of poetic mountains? This was the very country to shut one's eyes upon, without disparagement.' – Why so I did, but the postillions and boatmen obliged me to open them, as soon as they were closed. Four times was I shoved, out of my visions, into leaky boats, and towed across as many idle rivers. I

* The *Eclogues* of Virgil (70–19 B.C.) were pastoral poems modelled on the works of Theocritus (c. 310–c. 250 B.C.), the most important of the Greek Bucolic poets.

thought there was no end of these tiresome transits; and, when I reached my journey's end, was so compleatly jaded, that I almost believed Charon* would be the next aquatic I should have to deal with. The fair light of the morning (Tuesday, July 4th) was scarcely sufficient to raise my spirits, and I had left Bois le Duc a good way in arrears, before I was thoroughly convinced of my existence; when I looked through the blinds of the carriage, and saw nothing but barren plains and mournful willows, banks clad with rushes, and heifers so black and dismal, that Proserpine herself would have given them up to Hecate. I was near believing myself in the neighbourhood of a certain evil place, where I should be punished for all my croakings. We travelled at this rate, I dare say, fifteen miles, without seeing a single shed: at last, one or two miserable cottages appeared, darkened by heath, and stuck in a sandpit; from whence issued a half-starved generation, that pursued us a long while with their piteous wailings. The heavy roads and ugly prospects, together with the petulant clamours of my petitioners, made me quite uncharitable. I was in a dark, remorseless mood, which lasted me till we reached Brée, a shabby decayed town, encompassed by walls and ruined turrets. Having nothing to do, I straggled about them till night shaded the dreary prospects, and gave me an opportunity of imagining them, if I pleased, noble and majestic. Several of these waining edifices were invested with thick ivy: the evening was chill, and I crept under their coverts. Two or three brother owls were before me, but politely gave up their pretensions to the spot, and, as soon as I appeared, with a rueful whoop, flitted away to some deeper retirement. I had scarcely began to mope in tranquillity, before a rapid shower trickled amongst the clusters above me, and forced me to abandon my haunt. Returning in the midst of it to my inn, I hurried to bed; and was soon lulled to sleep by the storm . . . Starting up, I threw open the windows, and found it was eight o'clock, (Wednesday, July 5) and had hardly rubbed

---

* Charon was a Greek god of hell, the ferryman who carried souls over the river Styx to the underworld. Proserpine was a Roman goddess, the daughter of the earth-goddess, Ceres. She was abducted by Pluto, prince of the underworld. Hecate was another name for Proserpine during her stay in the underworld. Bulls were sacrificed to Hecate in Sicily.

my eyes, before beggars came limping from every quarter. I knew their plaguy voices but too well; and, that the same hubbub had broken my slumbers, and driven me from wisdom and riches to the regions of ignorance and poverty. The halt, the lame, and the blind, being restored by the miracle of a few stivers, to their functions, we breakfasted in peace, and, gaining the carriage, waded through the sandy deserts to Maestricht: our view however was considerably improved, for a league round the town, and presented some hills and pleasant valleys, smiling with crops of grain: here and there, green meadows, spread over with hay, varied the prospect, which the chirping of birds (the first I had heard for many a tedious day) amongst the barley, rendered me so chearful, that I began, like them, my exultations, and was equally thoughtless and serene. I need scarcely tell you, that, leaving the coach, I pursued a deep furrow between two extensive corn-fields, and reposed upon a bank of flowers, the golden ears waving above my head, and entirely bounding my prospect. Here I lay, in peace and sunshine, a few happy moments; contemplating the blue sky, and fancying myself restored to the valley at F[onthill], where I have past so many happy hours, shut out from the world, and concealed in the bosom of harvests ... I deserted my solitary bank, and proceeded on my journey. Maestricht abounds in Gothic churches, but contains no temple to Ceres. I was not sorry to quit it, after spending an hour unavoidably within its walls. Our road was conducted up a considerable eminence, from the summit of which we discovered a range of woody steeps, extending for leagues; beneath lay a winding valley, richly variegated, and lighted up by the Maese. The evening sun, scarcely gleaming through hazy clouds, cast a pale, tender hue upon the landscape, and the copses, still dewy with a shower that had lately fallen, diffused the most grateful fragrance. Flocks of sheep hung browsing on the acclivities, whilst a numerous herd were dispersed along the river's side. I staid so long, enjoying this pastoral scene, that we did not arrive at Liege, till the night was advanced, and the moon risen. Her interesting gleams were thrown away upon this ill-built, crowded city; and I grieved, that gates and fortifications prevented my breathing the fresh air of the surrounding mountains.

Next morning (July 6th) a zigzag road brought us, after many

descents and rises, to Spá. The approach, through a rocky vale, is
not totally devoid of picturesque merit; and, as I met no cabriolets*
or tituppings on the *chausée*, I concluded, that the waters were not
as yet much visited; and, that I should have their romantic environs
pretty much to myself. But, alas, how widely was I deceived! The
moment we entered, up flew a dozen sashes. Chevaliers de St Louis,†
meagre Marquises, and ladies of the scarlet order of Babylon, all
poked their heads out. In a few minutes, half the town was in motion;
taylors, confectioners, and barbers, thrusting bills into our hands,
with manifold grimaces and contortions. Then succeeded a *grand
entré* of *valets de place*, who were hardly dismissed before the lodging-
letters arrived, followed by somebody with a list of *les seigneurs* and
dames, as long as a Welsh pedigree. Half an hour was wasted in
speeches and recommendations; another passed, before we could
snatch a morsel of refreshment; they then finding I was neither
inclined to go to the ball, nor enter the land where Pharoah reigneth,‡
peace was restored, a few feeble bows were scraped, and I found
myself in perfect solitude. Taking advantage of this quiet moment, I
stole out of town, and followed a path cut in the rocks which brought
me to a young wood of oaks on their summits. Luckily I met no
saunterer; the gay vagabonds, it seems, were all at the assembly, as
happy as billiards and chit-chat could make them. It was not an
evening to tempt such folks abroad. The air was cool, and the sky
lowering, a melancholy cloud shaded the wild hills and irregular
woods at a distance. There was something so importunate in their
appearance, that I could not help asking their name, and was told
they were skirts of the forest of Ardenne, amongst whose enchanted
labyrinths the heroes of Boyardo and Ariosto§ roved formerly in
quest of adventures . .

*

* Light, one-horse chaises

† Holders of the *Croix St Louis*, awarded to officers and gentlemen for outstandingly
meritorious conduct on the field of battle. Also called the *feu* by reason of its bright
crimson ribbon.

‡ 'Pharoah' was contemporary slang for strong ale or beer. 'The land where Pharoah
reigneth' was most likely a tavern of some kind.

§ Matteomaria Boiardo (*c.* 1441–94), Italian poet, his unfinished *Orlando Innamorato*

Beckford described this place a day later in a letter to Cozens: 'Would to God that the memorable Fountains of Merlin were still attainable – I might then be happy with the hopes of forgetting a passion which preys upon my soul,' he wrote, referring to his infatuation for William Courtenay. 'I cannot break my chains – I struggle and the more attempts I make to shake them off the firmer they adhere to me. This wayward Love of mine makes me insensible to everything – I move feverishly from place to place – but it is in vain, it pursues me – pursues me with such swiftness! seizes upon me and marks me for its own.* O delicious Hours that are gone for ever,' he concluded, harking back to times with Courtenay at Powderham and Fonthill, 'your recollection is my sole comfort – I live alone by your remembrance.' [4]

. . . Away we went to Aix-la-Chapelle, about ten at night, and saw the mouldring turrets of that once illustrious capital, by the help of a candle and lantern. An old woman asked our names (for not a single soldier appeared) and, traversing a number of superannuated streets, without perceiving the least trace of Charlemain or his Paladins, we procured comfortable, though not magnificent apartments, and slept most unheroically sound, till it was time to set forwards for Dusseldorp.

July 8th

As we were driven out of town, I caught a glimpse of a grove, hemmed in by dingy buildings, where a few water-drinkers were sauntering along, to the sound of some rueful french-horns: the wan, greenish light, admitted through the foliage, made them look like unhappy souls, condemned to an eternal lounge for having trifled away their existence. It was not with much regret, that I left such a party behind; and, after experiencing the vicissitudes of good roads and rumbling pavements, found myself, towards the close of evening,

---

recast the legends of Charlemagne. Ludovico Aristo (1474–1533) finished the story in his *Orlando Furioso*.

* 'And Melancholy mark'd him for her own.' Beckford constantly identified with this line from Gray's 'Elegy', sometimes jocularly, but more often seriously.

upon the banks of the Rhine. Many wild ideas thronged in my mind, the moment I beheld this celebrated river. I thought of the vast regions through which it flows, and suffered my imagination to expatiate as far as its source. A red, variegated sky reflected from the stream, the woods trembling on its banks, and the spires of Nuys rising beyond them helped to amuse my fancy. Not being able to brook the confinement of the carriage, I left it to come over at its leisure; and, stepping into a boat, rowed along, at first, by the quivering osiers: then, launching out into the midst of the waters, I glided a few moments with the current, and, resting on my oars, listened to the hum of voices afar off, while several little skiffs, like canoes, glanced before my sight; concerning which, distance and the twilight allowed me to make a thousand fantastic conjectures. When I had sufficiently indulged these extravagant reveries, I began to cross over the river in good earnest; and being landed on its opposite margin, travelled forwards to the town. Nothing but the famous gallery of paintings, could invite strangers to stay a moment within its walls; more crooked streets, more indifferent houses, one seldom meets with: except soldiers, not a living creature moving about them; and at night, a compleat regiment of bugs 'marked me for their own' . . . the subject, suffering accordingly, was extremely rejoiced at flying from his persecutors to Cologne.

July 10th

Clouds of dust hindered my making any remarks on the exterior of this celebrated city . . . But, of what avail are stately palaces, broad streets, or airy markets, to a town which can boast of such a treasure, as the bodies of those three wise sovereigns, who were star-led to Bethlehem? Is not this circumstance enough to procure it every respect? I really believe so, from the pious and dignified contentment of its inhabitants. They care not a hair of an ass's ear, whether their houses be gloomy, and ill contrived; their pavements overgrown with weeds, and their shops with filthiness; provided the carcases of Gaspar, Melchior, and Balthazar might be preserved with proper decorum. Nothing, to be sure, can be richer, than the shrine which contains these precious relics. I payed my devotions before it, the moment I arrived; this step was inevitable; had I omitted it, not a soul in Cologne but would have cursed me for a Pagan. Do you not wonder at hearing of these venerable bodies, so far from their native country? I thought them snug in some Arabian pyramid, ten feet deep in spice; but, you see, one can never tell what is to become of one, a few ages hence . . . Very well; I think I had better stop in time, to tell you, without further excursion, that we set off after dinner for Bonn. Our road-side was lined with beggarly children, high convent-walls, and scarecrow crucifixes; lubberly monks, dejected peasants, and all the delights of Catholicism. Such scenery not engaging a great share of my attention, I kept gazing at the azure, irregular mountains, which bounded our view; and, in thought, was already transported to their summits . . . I entered the inn at Bonn; and was shewn into an apartment, which commands the chief front of the Elector's palace. You may guess how contemptible it appeared, to one just returned from the courts of fancy. In other respects, I saw it in a very favourable moment; for the twilight, shading the whole facade, concealed its plaistered walls and painted pillars; their pediments and capitals being tolerably well proportioned, and the range of windows beneath considerable, I gave the architect more credit than he deserved, and paced to and fro beneath the arcade, as pompously as if arrived at the Vatican; but the circumstance which rendered my walk in reality agreeable, was the prevalence of a delicious perfume. It was so dusky, that I was a minute or two seeking in vain the entrance of an orangery, from whence this reviving scent proceeded. At length I discovered it; and, passing under an arch, found myself in the midst of lemon and orange trees, now in the fullest blow, which form a continued grove before the palace, and extend, on each side of its grand portal, out of sight. A few steps separate this extensive terrace from a lawn, bordered by stately rows of beeches. Beyond, in the centre of this striking theatre rises a romantic assemblage of distant mountains, crowned with the ruins of castles, whose turrets, but faintly seen, were just such as you have created to compleat a prospect.* I was the only human being in the misty extent of the gardens, and

* Cozens taught his pupils by giving them set pieces to copy.

was happier in my solitude than I can describe. No noise disturbed its silence, except the flutter of moths and trickling of fountains . . .

July 11th

Let those who delight in picturesque country, repair to the borders of the Rhine, and follow the road which we took, from Bonn to Coblentz. In some places it is suspended like a cornice, above the waters; in others, it winds behind lofty steeps and broken acclivities, shaded by woods and cloathed with an endless variety of plants and flowers. Several green paths lead amongst this vegetation to the summits of the rocks, which often serve as the foundation of abbeys and castles, whose lofty roofs and spires, rising above the cliffs, impress passengers with ideas of their grandeur, that might probably vanish upon a nearer approach. Not chusing to lose any prejudice in their favour, I kept a respectful distance whenever I left my carriage, and walked on the banks of the river. Just before we came to Andernach, an antiquated town with strange morisco-looking towers, I spied a raft, at least three hundred feet in length, on which ten or twelve cottages were erected, and a great many people employed in sawing wood. The women sat spinning at their doors, whilst their children played among the water-lilies, that bloomed in abundance on the edge of the stream. A smoke, rising from one of these aquatic habitations, partially obscured the mountains beyond, and added not a little to their effect. Altogether, the scene was so novel and amusing, that I sat half an hour contemplating it, from an eminence under the shade of some leafy walnuts; and should like extremely to build a moveable village, people it with my friends, and so go floating about from island to island, and from one woody coast of the Rhine to another. Would you dislike such a party? I am much deceived, or you would be the first to explore the shades and promontories, beneath which we should be wafted along; but I don't think you would find Coblentz, where we were obliged to take up our night's lodging, much to your taste. 'Tis a mean, dirty assemblage of plaistered houses, striped with paint and set off with wooden galleries, in the beautiful taste of St Giles.* Above, on a rock, stands the palace of the Elector, which seems to be

* Presumably like a fair.

remarkable for nothing but situation. I did not bestow many looks on this structure whilst ascending the mountain, across which our road to Mayence conducted us.

July 12th

Having attained the summit, we discovered a vast irregular range of country, and advancing, found ourselves amongst downs, bounded by forests, and purpled with thyme. This sort of prospect extending for several leagues, I walked on the turf, and inhaled with avidity the fresh gales that blew over its herbage, till I came to a steep slope, overgrown with privet and a variety of luxuriant shrubs in blossom; there, reposing beneath the shade, I gathered flowers, listened to the bees, observed their industry, and idled away a few minutes with great satisfaction. A cloudless sky and bright sun-shine made me rather loth to move on, but the charms of the landscapes, increasing every instant, drew me forwards. I had not gone far, before a winding valley discovered itself, shut in by rocks and mountains, cloathed to their very summits with the thickest wood. A broad river, flowing at the base of the cliffs, reflected the impending vegetation, and looked so calm and grassy, that I was determined to be better acquainted with it. For this purpose, we descended by a zigzag path into the vale, and making the best of our way on the banks of the Lune (for so is the river called) came suddenly upon the town of Emms, famous in mineral story; where, finding very good lodgings, we took up our abode, and led an Indian life amongst the wilds and mountains. After supper, I walked on a smooth lawn by the river, to observe the moon journeying through a world of silver clouds, that lay dispersed over the face of the heavens. It was a mild genial evening: every mountain cast its broad shadow on the surface of the stream; lights twinkled afar off on the hills: they burnt in silence. All were asleep, except a female figure in white, with glow-worms shining in her hair.* She kept moving disconsolately about; sometimes I heard her sigh, and, if

* In Beckford's annotated copy of his Tour he has noted apropos: 'Twiss mentions that the Ladies at Cadiz – decorate themselves in the same manner when they take their Evening Walks on the Almeda – I have observed this custom in various parts of Spain and Portugal.'

apparitions sigh, this must have been an apparition. Upon my return, I asked a thousand questions, but could never obtain any information of the figure and its luminaries.

July 13th

The pure air of the morning invited me early to the hills. Hiring a skiff, I rowed about a mile down the stream, and landed on a sloping meadow, level with the waters, and newly mown. Heaps of hay still lay dispersed under the copses, which hemmed in on every side this little sequestered paradise. What a spot for a tent! I could encamp here for months, and never be tired. Not a day would pass by without discovering some new promontory, some untrodden pasture, some unsuspected vale, where I might remain among woods and precipices, lost and forgotton. I would give you, and two or three more, the clew of my labyrinth: nobody else should be conscious of its entrance. Full of such agreeable dreams, I rambled about the meads, scarce knowing which way I was going: sometimes a spangled fly led me astray, and, oftener, my own strange fancies. Between both, I was perfectly bewildered; and should never have found my boat again, had not an old German Naturalist, who was collecting fossils on the cliffs, directed me to it.

When I got home it was growing late, and I now began to perceive that I had taken no refreshment, except the perfume of the hay and a few wood strawberries . . .

July 14th

I have just made a discovery, that this place is as full of idlers and water-drinkers, as their Highnesses of Orange and Hesse Darmstadt can desire; for to them accrue all the profits of its salubrious fountains. I protest, I knew nothing of all this yesterday, so entirely was I taken up with rocks and meadows; no chance of meeting either card or billiard players in their solitudes. Both abound at Emms, where they hop and fidget from ball to ball, unconscious of the bold scenery in their neighbourhood, and totally insensible to its charms. They had no notion, not they, of admiring barren crags and precipices, where even the Lord would lose his way, as a coarse lubber, decorated with stars and orders, very ingeniously observed to me; nor could they form the least concept of any pleasure there was in climbing, like a goat, amongst the cliffs, and then diving into woods and recesses, where the sun never penetrated; where there were neither card-tables frequented, nor side-boards garnished; no *jambon de Mayence* in waiting; no supply of pipes, nor any of the commonest delights, to be met with in the commonest taverns . . .

I started up at seven in the morning of July 15th, ordered the horses, and set forward, without further dilemmas. Though it had thundered almost the whole night, the air was still clogged with vapours, the mountains bathed in humid clouds, and the scene I had so warmly admired no longer discernible. Proceeding along the edge of the precipices I had been forewarned of, for about an hour, and escaping that peril at least, we traversed the slopes of a rude healthy hill, in instantaneous expectation of foes and murderers . . . In this suspicious manner we journeyed through the forest, which had so recently been the scene of assaults and depredations. At length, after winding several restless hours amongst its dreary avenues, we emerged into open day-light. The sky cleared, a cultivated vale lay before us, and the evening sun, gleaming bright through the vapours, cast a chearful look upon some corn-fields, and seemed to promise better times. A few minutes more brought us to the village of Viesbaden, where we slept in peace and tranquillity.

July 16th

. . . we rose light and refreshed from our slumbers, and, passing through Mayence, Oppenheim and Worms, travelled gaily over the plain in which Manheim is situated. The sun set before we arrived there, and it was by the mild gleams of the rising moon, that I first beheld the vast electoral palace, and those long straight streets and neat white houses, which distinguish this elegant capital from almost every other.

Numbers of well-dressed people were amusing themselves with music and fire-works, in the squares and open spaces: other groups appeared conversing in circles before their doors, and enjoying the serenity of the evening. Almost every window bloomed with carnations; and we could hardly cross a street, without hearing the German flute . . .

July 20

After travelling a post or two, we came in sight of a green moor, with many insulated woods and villages, the Danube sweeping majestically along, and the city of Ulm rising upon its banks. The fields in its neighbourhood were overspread with cloths, bleaching in the sun, and waiting for barks [boats], which convey them down the great river, in ten days, to Vienna, and from thence, through Hungary, into the midst of the Turkish empire. I almost envied the merchants their voyage, and, descending to the edge of the stream, preferred my orisons to Father Danube, beseeching him to remember me to the regions through which he flows. I promised him an altar and solemn rites, should he grant my request, and was very idolatrous, till the shadows lengthening over the unlimited plains on his margin, reminded me, that the sun would be shortly sunk, and that I had still above fifteen miles to go. Gathering a purple iris that grew from the bank, I wore it to his honour; and have reason to fancy my piety was rewarded, as not a fly, or an insect, dared to buzz about me the whole evening . . . When the warm hues of the sky were gradually fading, and the distant thickets began to assume a deeper and more melancholy blue, I fancied a shape, like Thisbe,* shot swiftly along; and, sometimes halting afar off, cast an affectionate look upon her old master, that seemed to say, When you draw near the last inevitable hour, and the pale countries of Aneantsic† are stretched out before you, I will precede your footsteps, and guide them safe through the wild labyrinths which separate this world from yours. I was so possessed with the ideas, and so full of the remembrance of that poor, affectionate creature, whose miserable end you were the witness of, that I did not, for several minutes, perceive our arrival at Guntsberg

---

* A greyhound of Beckford's who had been torn to pieces by a mad dog.

† Aneantsic is Beckford's mis-transcription of Ataentsic, described by Father J. F. Lafitau, S.J., in his *Moeurs des sauvages Ameriquains, comparées aux moeurs des premiers temps* (Paris, 1724) as an American Indian goddess of the afterlife. This was a work Beckford referred to several times on his travels.

... Hurrying to bed, I seemed in my slumbers to pass that interdicted boundary which divides our earth from the region of Indian happiness. Thisbe ran nimbly before me; her white form glimmered amongst dusky forests; she led me into an infinitely spacious plain, where I heard vast multitudes discoursing upon events to come ... I awoke in tears, and could hardly find spirits enough to look around me, till we were driving through the midst of Augsburg.

July 21st

We dined, and rambled about this renowned city in the cool of the evening ... It happened to be a saint's day, and half the inhabitants of Augsburg were gathered together in the opening before their hall; the greatest numbers, especially the women, still exhibiting the very identical dresses which Hollar* engraved. My lofty gait imposed upon this primitive assembly, which receded to give me passage, with as much silent respect, as if I had really been the wise sovereign of Israel. When I got home, an execrable supper was served up to my majesty: I scolded in an unroyal style, and soon convinced myself I was no longer Solomon.

July 22nd

Joy to the Electors of Bavaria! for planting such extensive woods of fir in their dominions, as shade over the chief part of the road from Augsburg to Munich. Near the last-mentioned city, I cannot boast of the scenery changing to advantage. Instead of flourishing woods and verdure, we beheld a parched, dreary flat, diversified by fields of withering barley, and stunted avenues drawn formally across them; now and then a stagnant pool, and sometimes a dunghill, by way of regale. However, the wild rocks of the Tirol terminate the view, and to them imagination may fly, and walk amidst springs and lilies of her own creation. I speak from authority, having had the pleasure of anticipating an evening in this romantic style. Tuesday next is the grand fair, with horse-races and junkettings; a piece of news I was but too soon acquainted with; for the moment we entered the town,

* Wenceslaus Hollar (1607–77), Bohemian artist and engraver who spent much of his working life in England.

good-natured creatures from all quarters advised us to get out of it; since traders and harlequins had filled every corner of the place, and there was not a lodging to be procured. The inns, to be sure, were like hives of industrious animals, sorting their merchandise, and preparing their goods for sale. Yet, in spite of difficulties, we got possession of a quiet apartment.

July 23d

We were driven in the evening to Nymphenburg, the Elector's country palace, whose bosquets, jet d'eaux, and parterres, are the pride of the Bavarians. The principal platform is all of a glitter with gilded Cupids, and shining serpents, spouting at every pore. Beds of poppies, holy-oaks, scarlet lychnis, and the most flaming flowers, border the edge of the walks, which extend till the perspective meets, and swarm with ladies and gentlemen in party-coloured raiment . . . we joined Mr and Mrs T[revor],* and a party of fashionable Bavarians . . . and explored alley after alley, and pavilion after pavilion. Then, having viewed Pagotenburg, which is, as they told me, all Chinese; and Marienburg, which is most assuredly all tinsel; we paraded by a variety of fountains in full squirt, and though they certainly did their best (for many were set agoing on purpose) I cannot say I greatly admired them . . . Immediately after supper, we drove once more out of town, to a garden and tea-room, where all degrees and ages dance jovially to-gether till morning. Whilst one party wheel briskly away in the waltz, another amuse themselves in a corner, with cold meat and rhenish. That dispatched, out they whisk amongst the dancers, with an im-petuosity and liveliness I little expected to find in Bavaria. After turning round and round, with a rapidity that is quite inconceivable to an English dancer, the music changes to a slower movement, and then follows a succession of zigzag minuets, performed by old and young, straight and crooked, noble and plebeian, all at once, from one end of the room to the other. Tallow candles snuffing and stinking, dishes changing, heads scratching, and all sorts of performances going forwards at the same moment; the flutes, oboes, and bassoons snorting and grunting with peculiar emphasis; now fast, now slow, just as

* John Trevor (1749–1824) Minister-plenipotentiary at Munich.

variety commands, who seems to rule the ceremonial of this motley assembly, where every distinction of rank and privilege is totally forgotton ...

July 24th

Custom condemned us to visit the palace; which glares with looking-glass, gilding, and cut velvet. The chapel, though small, is richer than any thing Crœsus ever possessed, let them say what they will. Not a corner but shines with gold, diamonds and scraps of martyrdom studded with jewels. I had the delight of treading amethysts and the richest gems under foot; which, if you recollect, Apuleius* thinks such supreme felicity. Alas! I was quite unworthy of the honour, and had much rather have trodden the turf of the mountains ... The post is going out, and to-morrow we shall begin to mount the cliffs of the Tirol; but, don't be afraid of any long-winded epistles from their summits: I shall be too much fatigued in ascending them ...

July 25th

The noise of the people, thronging to the fair, did not allow me to slumber very long in the morning. When I got up, every street was crouded with Jews and mountebanks, holding forth and driving their bargains, in all the energetic vehemence of the German tongue. Vast quantities of rich merchandise glittered in the shops, as we passed along to the gates. Heaps of fruits and sweetmeats set half the grandams and infants in the place a cackling with felicity. Mighty glad was I to make my escape; and, in about an hour or two, we entered a wild tract of country, not unlike the skirts of a princely park. A little further on, stands a cluster of cottages, where we stopped to give our horses some bread, and were pestered with swarms of flies, most probably journeying to Munich fair, there to feast upon sugared tarts and bottle-noses. The next post brought us over hill and dale, grove and meadow, to a narrow plain, watered by rivulets and surrounded by cliffs, under which lies scattered the village of

* Apuleius, Lucius (c. 125–after 170). North African rhetorician and satirist whose most famous work is *The Golden Ass*.

Wollrasthausen ... Orchards of cherry-trees impend from the steeps above the village, which, to our certain knowledge, produce no contemptible fruit; for I can hardly think they eat better in the environs of Damascus. Having refreshed ourselves with this cooling juice, we struck into a grove of pines, the tallest and most flourishing, perhaps, we ever beheld. There seemed no end to these forests, save where little irregular spots of herbage, fed by cattle, intervened. Whenever we gained an eminence, it was only to discover more ranges of dark wood, variegated with meadows and glittering streams. White clover, and a profusion of sweet-scented flowers, cloath their banks; and beyond, rise hills, and rocks, and the mountains, piled upon one another, and fringed with fir to their topmost acclivities ... How we got over, the peasants best know; for without their assistance, I think our heavy carriage must needs have been stranded. Twilight drew on ... then ascending a steep hill, under a mountain, whose pines and birches rustled with the storm, we saw a little lake below. A deep azure haze veiled its eastern shore, and lowering vapours concealed the cliffs to the south; but over its western extremities a few transparent clouds, the remains of a struggling sun-set, were suspended, which streamed on the surface of the waters, and tinged with tender pink, the bow of a verdant promontory. I could not help fixing myself on the banks of the lake for several minutes, till this apparition was lost, and confounded with the shades of night. Looking round, I shuddered at a craggy mountain, cloathed in dark forests, and almost perpendicular, that was absolutely to be surmounted, before we could arrive at Wallersee. No house, not even a shed appearing, we were forced to ascend the peak, and penetrate these awful groves. Great praise is due to the directors of the roads across them; which considering their situation, are wonderfully fine ... As we advanced, in the thick shade, amidst the spray of torrents, and heard their loud roar in the chasm beneath, I could scarcely help thinking myself transported to the Grand Chartreuse; and began to conceive hopes of once more beholding St Bruno. But, though that venerable father did not vouchsafe an apparition, or call to me again from the depths of the dells, he protected his votary from nightly perils, and brought us to the banks of Wallersee lake. We saw lights gleam upon its shores, which directed us to a cottage, where we reposed after our toils, and were soon lulled to sleep by the fall of distant waters.

July 26th

The sun rose many hours before me; and, when I got up, was spangling the surface of the lake, which expands between steeps of wood, crowned by lofty crags and pinnacles . . .

After a few hours journey through the wilderness, we began to discover a wreath of smoke; and, presently, the cottage from whence it arose, composed of planks, and reared on the very brink of a precipice. Piles of cloven spruce-fir were dispersed before the entrance, on a little spot of verdure browsed by goats: near them sat an aged man with hoary whiskers, his white locks tucked under a fur-cap. Two or three beautiful children, their hair neatly braided, played around him, and a young woman, dressed in a short robe and polish-looking bonnet, peeped out of a wicket-window. I was so much struck with the exotic appearance of this sequestered family, that, crossing a rivulet, I clambered up to their cottage, and begged some refreshment. Immediately there was a contention among the children, who should be the first to oblige me. A little black-eyed girl succeeded, and brought me an earthen jug full of milk, with crumbled bread, and a platter of strawberries, fresh picked from the bank. I reclined in the midst of my smiling hosts, and spread my repast on the turf: never could I be waited upon with more hospitable grace. The only thing I wanted, was language to express my gratitude; and it was this deficiency which made me quit them so soon. The old man seemed visibly concerned at my departure; and his children followed me a long way down the rocks, talking in a dialect which passes all understanding, and waving their hands to bid me adieu. I had hardly lost sight of them, and regained the carriage, before we entered a forest of pines, to all apprearance without bounds, of every age and figure; some, feathered to the ground with flourishing branches; others, decayed into shapes like Lapland idols. I can imagine few situations more dreadful than to be lost at night amidst this confusion of trunks, hollow winds whistling amongst the branches, and strewing their cones below. Even at noon-day, I thought we should have never found our way out. At last, having descended a long avenue, endless perspectives opening on either side, we emerged into a valley bounded by swelling hills, divided into agreeable shady inclosures, where many herds were grazing. A rivulet flows along the pastures beneath; and, after winding through the village of Boidou, loses itself in a narrow pass, amongst the cliffs and precipices which rise above the cultivated slopes, and frame in this happy, pastoral region. All the plain was in sun-shine, the sky blue, and the heights illuminated, except one rugged peak with spires of rock, shaped not unlike the views I have seen of Sinai, and wrapped, like that sacred mount, in clouds and darkness. At the base of this tremendous mass, lies a neat hamlet, called Mittenvald, surrounded by thickets and banks of verdure, and watered by frequent springs, whose sight and murmurs were so re-viving in the midst of a sultry day, that we could not think of leaving their vicinity, but remained at Mittenvald, the whole evening. Our inn had long, airy galleries, and a pleasant balcony fronting the mountain. In one of these we dined upon trout, fresh from the rills, and cherries, just culled from the orchards that cover the slopes above.

July 27th

We pursued our journey to Inspruck, through some of the wildest scenes of wood and mountain that were ever traversed; the rocks now beginning to assume a loftier and more majestic appearance, and to glisten with snows. I had proposed passing a day or two at Inspruck; visiting the castle of Ambras, and examining Count Eysenberg's cabi-net, enriched with the rarest productions of the mineral kingdom, and a complete collection of the moths and flies peculiar to the Tirol; but, upon my arrival, the azure of the skies, and the brightness of the sunshine inspired me with an irresistible wish of hastening to Italy . . . Our road, the smoothest in the world (though hewn in the bosom of rocks) by its sudden turns and windings, gave us, every instant, opportunities of discovering new villages, and forests rising beyond forests; green spots in the midst of wood, high above on the moun-tains; and cottages, perched on the edge of promontories. Down, far below, in the chasm, amidst a confusion of pines and fragments of stone, rages the torrent Inn, which fills the country far and wide with a perpetual murmur. Sometimes we descended to its brink, and crossed over high bridges; sometimes, mounted half way up the cliffs, till its roar and agitation became, through distance, inconsiderable. After a long ascent, the shades of evening reposing in the vallies, and the upland snows still tinged with a vivid red, we reached Schönberg,* a village well worthy of its appellation; and then, twilight drawing over us, began to descend. We could now but faintly discover the opposite mountains veined with silver rills, when we came once more to the banks of the Inn. This turbulent stream accompanied us all the way to Steinach, and broke, by its continual roar, the stillness of the night, which had finished half its course, before we were settled to repose.

July 28th

I rose early, to scent the fragrance of the vegetation, bathed in a shower which had lately fallen; and, looking around me, saw nothing but crags hanging over crags, and the rocky shores of the stream, still dark with the shade of the mountains. The small opening in which Steinach is situated, terminates in a gloomy streight, scarce leaving room for the road and the torrent, which does not understand being thwarted, and will force its way, let the pines grow ever so thick, or the rocks be ever so considerable. Notwithstanding the forbidding air of this narrow dell, industry has contrived to enliven its steeps with habitations; to raise water by means of a wheel; and to cover the surface of the rocks with soil. By this means, large crops of oats and flax are produced, and most of the huts have gardens adjoining, which are filled with poppies, seeming to thrive in this parched situation; . . . The further we advanced in the dell, the larger were the plantations which discovered themselves. For what purpose these gaudy flowers meet with such encouragement, I had neither time nor language to enquire; the mountaineers stuttering a gibberish, unintelligible, even to Germans. Probably, opium is extracted from them . . .

* 'Beautiful mountain'.

July 29th

We proceeded over fertile mountains to Bolsano. Here, first, I noticed the rocks cut into terraces, thick set with melons, and Indian corn; gardens of fig-trees and pomegranates hanging over walls, clustered with fruit. In the evening, we perceived several further indications of approaching Italy; and, after sun-set, the Adige, rolling its full tide between precipices, which looked awful in the dusk. Myriads of fire-flies sparkled amongst the shrubs on the bank. I traced the course of these exotic insects by their blue light, now rising to the summits of the trees, now sinking to the ground, and associating with vulgar glow-worms. We had opportunities enough to remark their progress, since we travelled all night; such being my impatience to reach the promised land! Morning dawned, just as we saw Trent dimly before us. I slept a few hours, then set out again, (July 30th) after the heats were in some degree abated; and, leaving Bergine, (where the peasants were feasting before their doors in their holiday dresses, with red pinks stuck in their ears in lieu of rings, and their necks surrounded with coral of the same colour) we came, through a woody valley, to the banks of a lake, filled with the purest and most transparent water, which loses itself in shady creeks, amongst hills, robed with verdure, from their base to their summits. The shores present one continual shrubbery, interspersed with knots of larches and slender almonds, starting from the underwood. A cornice of rock runs round the whole, except where the trees descend to the very brink, and dip their boughs in the water. It was five o'clock when I caught the sight of this unsuspected lake, and the evening shadows stretched nearly across it. Gaining a very rapid ascent, we looked down upon its placid bosom, and saw several airy peaks rising above the tufted foliage of the groves around. I quitted the contemplation of them with regret; and, in a few hours, arrived at Borgo di Valsugano, the scenes of the lake still present before the eye of my fancy.

July 31st

My heart beat quick, when I saw some hills, not very distant, which, I was told, lay in the Venetian state; and I thought an age, at least, had elapsed before we were passing their base. The road was never formed to delight an impatient traveller; loose pebbles and rolling stones render it, in the highest degree, tedious and jolting. I should not have spared my execrations, had it not traversed a picturesque valley, overgrown with juniper, and strewed with fragments of rock, precipitated, long since, from the surrounding eminences, blooming with cyclamens. I clambered up several of these crags to gather the flowers I have just mentioned, and found them deliciously scented. Fritillarias, and the most gorgeous flies, many of which I here noticed for the first time, were fluttering about, and expanding their wings in the sun. There is no describing the numbers I beheld, nor their gayly varied colouring. I could not find in my heart to destroy their felicity; to scatter such bright plumage, and snatch them for ever, from the realms of light and flowers. Had I been less compassionate, I should have gained credit with that respectable corps, the torturers of butterflies; and might, perhaps, have enriched their cabinets with some unknown captives. However, I left them imbibing the dews of heaven, in free possession of their native rights; and, having changed horses at Tremolano, entered, at length, my long-desired Italy. The pass is rocky and tremendous, guarded by a fortress (Covalo) in possession of the Empress Queen,* and only fit, one should think, to be inhabited by her eagles . . . the Brenta foaming and thundering below. Beyond, the rocks began to be mantled with vines and gardens. Here and there a cottage, shaded with mulberries, made its appearance; and we often discovered, on the banks of the river, ranges of white buildings, with courts and awnings, beneath which vast numbers were employed in manufacturing silk. As we advanced, the stream gradually widened, and the rocks receded; woods were more frequent, and cottages thicker strewn. About five in the evening, we had left the country of crags and precipices, of mists and cataracts, and were entering the fertile territory of the Bassanese. It was now I beheld groves of olives, and vines clustering the summits of the tallest elms; pomegranates in every garden, and vases of citron and orange before almost every door. The softness and transparency of the air, soon told me I was arrived in happier climates; and I felt sensations of joy and novelty run through my veins . . . Peasants were returning homeward from

* Maria Theresa of Austria, 1717–80.

the cultivated hillocks and corn-fields, singing as they went, and calling to each other over the hills; whilst the women were milking goats before the wickets of the cottages, and preparing their country fare. I left them enjoying it, and soon beheld the ancient ramparts and cypresses of Bassano; whose classic appearance recalled the memory of former times, and answered exactly the ideas I had pictured to myself of Italian edifices. Though encompassed by walls and turrets, neither soldiers nor custom-house officers start out from their concealments, to question and molest a weary traveller; for such are the blessings of the Venetian state, at least of the Terra Firma provinces, that it does not contain, I believe, above four regiments. Istria, Dalmatia, and the maritime frontiers, are more formidably guarded, as they touch, you know, the whiskers of the Turkish empire. Passing under a Doric gateway, we crossed the chief part of this town in the way to our locanda,* pleasantly situated, and commanding a level green, where people walk and eat ices by moonlight. On the right, the Franciscan church and convent, half hid in the religious gloom of pines and cypress; to the left, a perspective of walls and towers rising from the turf, and marking it, when I arrived, with long shadows; in front where the lawn terminates, meadow, wood and garden run quite to the base of the mountains. Twilight coming on, this beautiful spot swarmed with people, sitting in circles upon the grass, refreshing themselves with cooling liquors, or lounging upon the bank beneath the towers. They looked so free and happy, that I longed to be acquainted with them; and, by the interposition of a polite Venetian (who, though a perfect stranger, shewed me the most engaging marks of attention) was introduced to a group of the principal inhabitants. Our conversation ended in a promise to meet the next evening at a country house about a league from Bassano, and then to return together, and sing to the praise of Pachierotti,† their idol, as well as mine . . .

---

* A lodging-house, or inn.
† Gasparo Pacchierotti (1740–1821), the greatest *castrato* of his day. Beckford had met him in London shortly before leaving for the continent. They were to become dear friends.

August 1st

The whole morning, not a soul stirred who could avoid it. Those, who were so active and lively the night before, were now stretched languidly upon their couches. Being to the full as idly disposed, I sat down and wrote some of this dreaming epistle; then feasted upon figs and melons; then got under the shade of the cypress, and slumbered till evening, only waking to dine and take some ice. The sun declining apace, I hastened to my engagement at Mosolente (for so is the villa called) placed on a verdant hill, encircled by others as lovely, and consisting of three light pavilions connected by porticos; just such as we admire in the fairy scenes of an opera. A vast flight of steps leads to the summit, where Signora Roberti and her friends received me, with a grace and politeness that can never want a place in my memory . . . Behind the villa, a tumble of hillocks present themselves in variety of forms, with dips and hollows between, scattered over with leafy trees and vines dangling in continued garlands. I gazed on this rural view till it faded in the dusk; then, returning to Bassano, repaired to an illuminated hall, and had the felicity of hearing La Signora Roberti sing . . . As soon as she had ended, and that I could hear no more those affecting sounds, which had held me silent and almost breathless for several moments, a band of various instruments, stationed in the open street, began a lively symphony, which would have delighted me at any other time; but, now, I wished them a thousand leagues away, so melancholy an impression did the air I had been listening to, leave on my mind. At midnight, I took leave of my obliging hosts, who were just setting out for Padua. They gave me a thousand kind invitations, and I hope some future day to accept them.

August 2d

Our route to Venice lay winding about the variegated plains I had surveyed from Mosolente; and, after dining at Treviso, we came, in two hours and a half, to Mestre, between grand villas, and gardens peopled with statues. Embarking our baggage at the last-mentioned place, we stepped into a gondola, whose even motion was very agreeable after the jolts of a chaise. Stretched beneath the awning, I enjoyed my ease, the freshness of the gales, and the sight of the waters. We were soon out of the canal of Mestre, terminated by an isle, which contains a cell dedicated to the holy virgin, peeping out of a thicket, from whence spire up two tall cypresses. Its bells tingled, as we passed along and dropped some paolis [coins] into a net tied at the head of a pole, stretched out to us for the purpose. As soon as we had doubled the cape of this diminutive island, an azure expanse of sea opened to our view, the domes and towers of Venice rising from its bosom. Now we began to distinguish Murano, St Michele, St Giorgio in Alga, and several other islands, detached from the grand cluster, which I hailed as old acquaintance; innumerable prints and drawings having long since made their shapes familiar. Still gliding forwards, the sun casting his last gleams across the waves, and reddening the distant towers, we every moment distinguished some new church or palace in the city, suffused with the evening rays, and reflected with all their glow of colouring from the surface of the waters ... We were now drawing very near the city; and a confused hum began to interrupt the evening stillness; gondolas were continually passing and repassing, and the entrance of the canal Reggio, with its stir and bustle, lay before us. Our gondoliers turned, with much address, through a croud of boats and barges that blocked up the way, and rowed smoothly by the side of a broad pavement, covered with people in all dresses, and of all nations. Leaving the Palazzo Pesaro, ... we were soon landed before the Leon Bianco, which, being situated in one of the broadest parts of the grand canal, commands a most striking assemblance of buildings ... At one end of this grand perspective, appears the Rialto; the sweep of the canal conceals the other. The rooms of our hotel are as spacious and cheerful, as I could desire; a lofty hall, or rather gallery, painted with grotesque, in a very good style, perfectly clean, floored with a marbled stucco, divides the house, and admits a refreshing current of air. Several windows near the ceiling, look into this vast apartment, which serves in lieu of a court, and is rendered perfectly luminous by a glazed arcade, thrown open to catch the breezes. Through it, I passed to a balcony, which impends over the canal, and is twined round with plants forming a grand festoon, and springing from two large vases of orange-trees placed at each end. Here I established myself, to enjoy the cool, and observe, as well as the dusk would permit, the variety of figures shooting by in their gondolas. As night approached, innumerable tapers glimmered through the awnings before the windows. Every boat had its lantern, and the gondolas, moving rapidly along, were followed by tracks of light, which gleamed and played on the waters. I was gazing at these dancing fires, when the sounds of music were wafted along the canals, and, as they grew louder and louder, an illuminated barge, filled with musicians, issued from the Rialto, and, stopping under one of the palaces, began a serenade, which was clamorous, and suspended all conversation in the galleries and porticos; till, rowing slowly away, it was heard no more. The gondoliers catching the air, imitated its cadences, and were answered by others at a distance, whose voices, echoed by the arch of the bridge, acquired a plaintive and interesting tone. I retired to rest, full of the sound, and, long after I was asleep, the melody seemd to vibrate in my ear.

August 3d

It was not five o'clock before I was roused, by a loud din of voices and splashing of water, under my balcony. Looking out, I beheld the grand canal so entirely covered with fruits and vegetables, on rafts and in barges, that I could scarcely distinguish a wave. Loads of grapes, peaches, and melons arrived, and disappeared in an instant; for every vessel was in motion, and the crowds of purchasers hurrying from boat to boat, formed one of the liveliest pictures imaginable ... I procured a gondola, laid in my provision of bread and grapes, and was rowed under the Rialto, down the grand canal, to the marble steps of S. Maria della Salute, erected by the senate in performance of a vow to the holy Virgin, who begged off a terrible pestilence in 1630. I gazed, delighted with its superb frontispiece and dome, relieved by a clear blue sky. To criticize columns, or pediments of the different façades, would be time lost; since one glance upon the worst view [painting] that has been taken of them, conveys a far better idea than the most elaborate description. The great bronze portal opened, whilst I was standing on the steps which lead to it, and discovered the interior of the dome, where I expatiated in solitude; no mortal appearing, except an old priest, who trimmed the lamps, and muttered a prayer before the high altar, still wrapped in shadows. The sun beams began to strike against the windows of the cupola, just as I left the church, and was wafted across the waves to the spacious platform in front of St Giorgio Maggiore, by far the most perfect and beautiful edifice my eyes ever beheld. When my first transport was a little subsided, and I had examined the graceful design of each particular ornament, and united the just proportion and grand effect of the whole in my mind, I planted my umbrella on the margin of the sea, and reclining under its shade, my feet dangling over the waters, viewed the vast range of palaces, of porticos, of towers, opening on every side, and extending out of sight . . .

That night he met the woman who was to throw open the doors of the Venetian salons to him. Giustiniana Wynne d'Orsini-Rosenberg (1727–91) the 'M. de R.' of Beckford's journal, was then fifty-three, the slightly raffish widow of an elderly Austrian diplomat. She came from the noted Welsh family of Wynne of Capel Protrew, had at one time known Casanova, was an inveterate gambler, and dabbled fashionably in literature and philosophy. The Begum would not have approved. From now on it was Giustiniana who supervised Beckford's Venetian experience, showed him the galleries, palaces, churches, bore him off to concerts, and introduced him, with unlooked-for consequences, to people of his own age.

. . . She very obligingly presented me to some of the most distinguished of the Venetian families, at their great casino which looks into the piazza, and consists of five or six rooms, fitted up in a gay flimsy taste, neither rich nor elegant; where were a great many lights, and a great many ladies negligently dressed, their hair falling very freely about them, and innumerable adventures written in their eyes. The gentlemen were lolling upon the sofas, or lounging about the apartments. The whole assembly seemed on the verge of gaping [yawning], till coffee was carried round. The magic beverage diffused a temporary animation; and, for a moment or two, conversation moved on with a degree of pleasing extravagance; but the flash was soon dissipated, and nothing remained save cards and stupidity . . .

August 4th

The heats were so excessive in the night, that I thought myself
several times on the point of suffocation, tossed about like a wounded
fish, and dreamt of the devil and Senegal. Towards sunrise, a faint
breeze restored me to life and reason. I slumbered till late in the day;
and, the moment I was fairly awake, ordered my gondolier to row out
to the main ocean, that I might plunge into its waves, and hear and
see nothing but waters round me. We shot off, wound amongst a
number of sheds, shops, churches, casinos, and palaces, growing
immediately out of the canals, without any apparent foundation. No
quay, no terrace, not even a slab is to be seen before the doors; one
step brings you from the hall into the bark, and the vestibules of the
stateliest structures lie open to the waters, and level with them. I
observed several, as I glided along, supported by rows of well-
proportioned pillars, adorned with terms [statues] and vases, beyond
which the eye generally discovers a grand court, and sometimes a
garden. In about half an hour, we had left the thickest cluster of isles
behind, and, coasting the palace of St Mark opposite to San Giorgio
Maggiore, whose elegant frontispiece was painted on the calm waters,
launched into the blue expanse of sea . . . I ran to the smooth sands,
extending to both sides out of sight, cast off my clothes, and dashed
into the waves; which were coursing one another with a gentle motion,
and breaking lightly on the shores. The tide rolled over me as I lay
floating about, buoyed up by the water, and carried me wheresoever
it listed . . . My ears filled with murmuring undecided sounds; my
limbs stretched languidly on the surf, rose, or sunk, just as it swelled
or subsided. In this passive, senseless state I remained, till the
sun cast a less intolerable light, and the fishing vessels, lying out in
the bay at great distance, spread their sails and were coming
home . . .

*But behind such a calm entry in the journal an altogether different
state of affairs prevailed. By now, thanks to the indefatigable Giustiniana, Beckford had been introduced, and absorbed, into the aristocratic Cornaro family. There were two sisters, and a brother of his
own age, and almost instantly, one of the sisters became so wildly*

infatuated with Beckford that she determined to dispatch her husband with poison in order to be free to roam Europe with their fascinating new English friend. By some oversight she imbibed the potion herself, fortunately with little effect. 'Never shall I forget a night scene which took place – most appropriately one stormy night – at the Cornaro palace . . .' added Beckford later by way of a footnote. 'The Vendramin upbraided me with loving her sister. I told her I did not, but that my friendship for her brother was unbounded. She answered with a convulsive gasp, "Respiro – I have nothing to do with friendship, but if you dare to return my sister's frantic passion I will be revenged, and terribly." '⁵ Of his friendship with the Cornaro boy he wrote to Louisa Beckford that, 'It was a passion of mind resembling those generous attachments we venerate in ancient history, and Holy writ. What David felt towards the brother of his heart, the son of Saul, I experienced towards the person here alluded to.'⁶

August 18th

It rains; the air is refreshed, and I have courage to resume my pen, which the sultry weather had forced to lie dormant so long. I like this odd town of Venice, and find every day some new amusement in rambling about its innumerable canals and alleys. Sometimes, I go and pry about the great church of Saint Mark, and examine the variety of marbles, and mazes of delicate sculpture, with which it is covered. The cupola, glittering with gold, mosaic, and paintings of half the wonders in the Apocalypse, never fails transporting me to the period of the Eastern empire. I think myself in Contantinople, and expect Michael Paleologus* with all his train. One circumstance alone, prevents my observing half the treasures of the place, and holds down my fancy, just springing into the air: I mean the vile stench, which exhales from every recess and corner of the edifice, and which all the altars cannot subdue. When oppressed by this noxious atmosphere, I run up the Campanile in the piazza; and, seating myself amongst the pillars of the gallery, breathe the fresh gales which blow from the Adriatic; survey at my leisure all Venice beneath me, with its azure sea, white sails, and long tracks of islands, shining in the

* Eastern Roman Emperor (1234–82).

sun. Having thus laid in a provision of wholesome breezes, I brave the vapours of the canals, and venture into the most curious, and musky quarters of the city, in search of Turks and Infidels, that I may ask as many questions as I please about Damascus and Suristan, those happy countries, which nature has covered with roses. Asiatics find Venice very much to their liking; and all those I conversed with, allowed its customs and style of living had a good deal of conformity to their own. The eternal lounging in coffee-houses, and sipping of sorbets, agrees perfectly well with the inhabitants of the Ottoman empire, who stalk about in their proper dresses, and smoke their own exotic pipes, without being stared and wondered at, as in most other European capitals ... Scarce one evening have I failed to remark the changeful scenery of the clouds, and to fill my mind with recollections of primeval days, and happier ages. Night generally surprizes me in the midst of my reveries; I return, lulled in my gondola by the murmur of waters, pass about an hour with M. de R. whose imagination and sensibility almost equal your own; then, retire to sleep, and dream of the Euganeans.

Euganeans? That early pastoral people, driven, so Livy tells us, from their lands by the Trojans? One wonders. It seems that even the robust Giustiniana was growing apprehensive as Beckford, with a dreadful single-mindedness, pursued his affair with young Cornaro. He had already caused scandal by giving public vent to his infatuation, and had presented the boy with his portrait. Giustiniana and her own in-amorato, the biddable Count Benincasa, now began in earnest, and far too late, to divert Beckford with less inflaming distractions.

August 27th
I have just returned from visiting the isles of Burano, Torcello, and Mazorbo ... Beyond them, on the coast of the Lagunes, rose the once populous city of Altina, with its six stately gates ... Two of the islands, Constanziaco and Amiano, that are imagined to have contained the bowers and gardens of the Altinatians, have sunk beneath the waters, those which remain, are scarcely worth to rise above their surface. Though I was persuaded little was left to be seen above

ground, I could not deny myself the imaginary pleasure of treading a corner of the earth, once so adorned and cultivated; and of walking over the roofs, perhaps, of concealed halls, and undiscovered palaces. M[adame] de R[osenberg], to whom I communicated my ideas, entered at once into the scheme; hiring therefore a peiotte [small boat], we took some provisions and music (to us equal necessaries of life) and launched into the canal, between Saint Michael and Murano. The waves coursed each other with violence; and dark clouds hung over the grand sweep of northern mountains, whilst the west smiled with azure, and bright sunshine. Thunder rolled awfully at a distance, and those white and greyish birds, the harbingers of storms, flitted frequently before our bark. For some moments we were in doubt, whether to proceed; but, as we advanced by a little dome in the isle of Saint Michael, shaped like an antient temple, the sky cleared, and the ocean subsiding by degrees, soon presented a tranquil expanse, across which we were smoothly wafted. Our instruments played several delightful airs, that called forth the inhabitants of every island, and held them silent, and spell-bound, on the edge of their quays and terraces, till we were out of hearing. Leaving Murano far behind, Venice and its world of turrets, began to sink on the horizon, and the low, desert isles beyond Mazorbo, to lie stretched out before us.

Now we beheld vast wastes of purple flowers, and could distinguish the low hum of the insects which hover above them; such was the silence of the place. Coasting along these solitary fields, we wound amongst several serpentine canals, bordered by gardens of figs and pomegranates, with neat, Indian looking inclosures of cane and reed: an aromatic plant clothes the margin of the waters, which the people justly dignify with the title of marine incense. It proved very serviceable in subduing a musky odour, which attacked us the moment we landed; and which proceeds from serpents that lurk in the hedges. These animals, say the gondoliers, defend immense treasures, which lie buried under the ruins ... we walked over a soil, composed of crumbling bricks and cement, to the cathedral; whose arches, turned on the antient Roman principle, convinced us that it dates as high as the sixth or seventh century ... By the time we had examined every nook and corner of this singular edifice, and caught perhaps some small portion of sanctity, by sitting in San Lorenzo's chair, dinner was prepared in a neighbouring convent; and the nuns, allured by the sound of our flutes and oboes, peeped out of their cells, and shewed themselves by dozens at the grate. Some few agreeable faces and interesting eyes enlivened the dark sisterhood: all seemed to catch a gleam of pleasure from the music: two or three of them, probably the last immured, let fall a tear, and suffered the recollection of the world and its prophane joys to interrupt, for a moment, their sacred tranquillity. We staid till the sun was low and the breezes blew cool from the ocean on purpose that they might listen as long as possible to a harmony, which seemed to issue, as the old abbess expressed herself, from the gates of paradise a-jar ... In two hours, we were safely landed at the Fondamenti Nuovi, and went immediately to the Mendicanti, where they were performing the oratorio of Sisera ... The sight of the orchestra still makes me smile. You know, I suppose, it is entirely of the female gender; and that nothing is more common, than to see a delicate white hand journeying across an enormous double bass; or a pair of roseate cheeks puffing with all their efforts at a french-horn. Some of them are grown old and Amazonian, who have abandoned their fiddles and their lovers, take vigorously to the kettle-drum; and one poor limping lady, who had been crossed in love, now makes an admirable figure on the bassoon. Good night! I am quite exhausted with composing a chorus for these same Amazons ...

Eight days later he left Venice in company with Giustiniana, her Count, and his own 'pagan idol' as he was now calling Cornaro.

September 4th
I was sorry to leave Venice, and regretted my peaceful excursions upon the Adriatic ... About an hour's rowing from the isle of St Giorgio in Alga, brought up to the shores of Fusina, right opposite the opening, where the Brenta mixes with the sea. The river flows calmly between banks of verdure, crowned by poplars, with vines twining round every stalk, and depending from tree to tree, in beautiful festoons. Beds of mint and flowers, clothe the brink of the stream except where a tall growth of reeds and oziers lift themselves to the

breezes. I heard their whispers as we glided along; and, had I been alone, might have told you what they said to me; but such aerial oracles must be approached in solitude. The morning continued to lower as we advanced; scarce a wind ventured to breathe: all was still and placid as the surface of the Brenta. No sound struck my ears, except the bargemen hollowing to open the sluices, and deepen the water. As yet I had not perceived an habitation; no other objects than green meads and fields of Turkish corn, shaded with vines and poplars, met my eyes wherever I turned them. Our navigation, the tranquil streams and cultivated banks, in short the whole landscape, had a sort of Chinese cast, which led me into Quang-Si and Quang-Tong. The variety of canes, reeds, and blossoming rushes shooting from the slopes, confirmed my fancies; and when I beheld the yellow nenupha expanding its broad leaves to the current, I thought of the Tao-Sé, and venerated one of the chief ingredients in their beverage of immortality. Landing where this magic vegetation appeared most luxuriant, I cropped the flowers ... Whilst I was thus agreeably employed, it began to rain, and the earth to exhale a fresh reviving odour, highly grateful to one who had been so long confined to walls and waters. After breathing nothing but the essence of canals, and the flavours of the Rialto; after the jinglings of bells, and brawls of the gondoliers, imagine how agreeable it was, to scent the perfume of clover; to tread a springing herbage, and to listen in silence to the showers, pattering amongst the leaves ... Passing the great sluices, whose gates opened with a thundering noise, we continued our course along the peaceful Brenta, winding its broad full stream through impenetrable copses, surmounted by tall waving poplars. Day was about to close when we reached Fiesso; and, it being a misty evening, I could scarcely distinguish the pompous façade of the Pisani palace. That, where we supped, looked upon a broad mass of foliage, which I contemplated with pleasure, as it sunk in the dusk. We walked a long while, under a pavilion stretched before the entrance, breathing the freshness of the wood after the shower, and hearing the drops trickle down the awning above our heads. The Galuzzi* sung some of her

* Galuzzi Ferandini was the daughter of Giovanni Ferandini (1705-93), composer and teacher.

father Ferandini's compositions, with a fire, an energy, an expression, that, one moment, raised me to a pitch of heroism, and the next, dissolved me in tears. Her cheek was flushed with inspiration; her eyes glistened; the whole tone of her countenance was like that of a person rapt and inspired. I forgot both time and place, whilst she was breathing forth such celestial harmony. The night stole imperceptibly away, and morning dawned, before I awoke from my trance ... I loathed the light of the morning star, which summoned me to depart; and, if I may express myself so poetically, 'cast many a longing, ling'ring look behind'.

Young Cornaro's sister also sang that evening. Beckford wrote how Marietta 'threw quick around her the glancing fires of genius', sending him and the young man he loved, 'that one for whom I felt the most enthusiastic friendship,' 'into a strange delirium'. The aria Marietta sang, and which he never forgot, was 'Pur ne sonno almen talora' from Gluck's Orfeo, and Beckford, for whom the words conveyed a special meaning, translated them thus:

> When sleep its magic balm instils,
> The form I love my vision fills;
> Swift flies each torturing pain.
> Imperious God, Thy justice prove,
> Ah, realise the dream of love
> Or wake me not again.[7]

It was a vision that was to haunt him relentlessly for the remainder of the Tour. 'Alas, I can find no distractions,' he wrote to Count Benincasa. 'Fate gives me no peace. Landscapes and the splendours of the setting sun have lost their effect ... One image alone possess me and pursues me in a terrible way. In vain do I throw myself into Society this image forever starts up before me. In vain do I try to come up to the great expectations framed of me – my words are cut short and I am halted in mid-career. This unique object is all I hope for – I am dead to anything else ...'[8]

September 5th

The glow and splendor of the rising sun, for once in my life, drew little of my attention. I was too deeply plunged in my reveries, to notice the landscape which lay before me; and the walls of Padua presented themselves, some time, ere I was aware. At any other moment, how sensibly should I have been affected with their appearance! How many ideas of Antenor* and his Trojans, would have thronged into my memory! but now, I regarded the scene with indifference; and passed many a palace, and many a woody garden, with my eyes rivetted to the ground. The first object that appeared upon lifting them up, was a confused pile of spires and cupolas, dedicated to blessed Saint Anthony, who betook himself to the conversion of fish, after the heretics would lend no ear to his discourses. You are too well apprized of the veneration I have always entertained for this ingenious preacher, to doubt that I immediately repaired to his shrine, and offered up my little orizons before it. Mine was a disturbed spirit; and required all the balm of Saint Anthony's kindness, to appease it. Perhaps, you will say, I had better gone to bed, and applied myself to my sleepy friend, the pagan divinity. 'Tis probable that you are in the right; but I could not retire to rest, without venting some portion of effervescence, in sighs and supplications. The nave was filled with decrepit women and feeble children, kneeling by baskets of vegetables and other provisions; which, by good Anthony's interposition, they hoped to sell advantageously, in the course of the day. Beyond these, nearer the choir, and in a gloomier part of the edifice, knelt a row of rueful penitents, smiting their breasts, and lifting their eyes to heaven. Further on, in front of the dark recess, where the sacred relics are deposited, a few desperate, melancholy sinners lay prostrate. To these I joined myself, and fell down on the steps before the shrine.† The sun-beams had not yet penetrated into this religious quarter; and the only light it

---

* A Trojan prince who after the fall of Troy fled to Italy and founded Padua.

† As so often with Beckford he joked and yet he did not. There is no doubt that he was suffering guilt and anguish over the Cornaro affair, feeling it to be that 'soft alluring of a criminal passion' which Lady Hamilton would warn him against when he got to Naples.

received, proceeded from the golden lamps, which hung in clusters round the sanctuary. A lofty altar, decked with superstitious prodigality, conceals the holy pile from profane glances. Those, who are profoundly touched with its sanctity, may approach, and, walking round, look through the crevices of the tomb, and rub their rosaries against the identical bones of St Anthony; which, it is observed, exude a balsamic odour. But, supposing a traveller ever so heretical, I would advise him by no means to neglect this pilgrimage; since every part of the recess he visits, is decorated with the most exquisite sculptures. Sansovino and the best artists, have vied with each other in carving the alto-relievos of the arcade; which, for design and execution, would do honour to the sculptors of antiquity. Having observed these treasures, with much less exactness than they merited, and acted, perhaps, too capital a part among the devotees, I hastened to the inn, luckily, hard by, and one of the best I am acquainted with. Here I soon fell asleep, in defiance of sunshine. 'Tis true, my slumbers were not a little agitated. Saint Anthony had been deaf to my prayer, and I still found myself a frail, infatuated mortal . . .

September 6th

At Padua I was too near the last, and one of the most celebrated abodes of Petrarch, to make the omission of a visit excuseable; had I not been in a disposition to render such a pilgrimage peculiarly pleasing.* I set forwards from Padua after dinner, so as to arrive some time before sun-set. Nothing could be finer than the day; and I had every reason to promise myself a serene and delicious hour, before the sun might go down. I put the poems of Petrarch into my pocket; and, as my road lay chiefly through lanes, planted on either side with mulberries and poplars, from which vines hung dangling in careless festoons, I found many a bowering shade, where I sat, at intervals, to indulge my pensive humour, over some ejaculatory sonnet; as the pilgrim, on his journey to Loretto, reposes here and there, to offer his prayers and meditations to the Virgin. In little more than an hour and half, I found myself in the midst of the Euganean hills, and, after

* Presumably since Petrarch and Beckford both suffered from hopeless love!

winding almost another hour amongst them, I got, before I was well aware, into the village of Arqua. Nothing can be more sequestered or obscure, than its situation. It had rather a deserted appearance; several of its houses being destitute of inhabitants, and crumbling into ruins. Two or three of them, however, exhibited antient towers, richly mantled with ivy, and surrounded with cypress, that retained the air of having once belonged to persons of consideration. Their present abandoned state, nourished the melancholy idea with which I entered the village. Could one approach the last retreat of genius, and not look for some glow of its departed splendor? . . . In a letter to one of his friends, written about this period of his life, he says:

I pass the greatest part of the year in the country, which I have always preferred to cities: I read; I write; I think: thus, my life, and my pleasures are like those of youth. I take pains to hide myself; but I cannot escape visits: it is an honour which displeases and wearies me. In my little house on the Euganean hills, I hope to pass my few remaining days in tranquillity, and to have always before my eyes my dead, or my absent friends.

I was musing on these circumstances as I walked along the village, till a venerable old woman, seated at her door with her distaff in her hand, observing me, soon guessed the cause of my excursion; and offered to guide me to Petrarch's house. The remainder of my way was short, and well amused by my guide's enthusiastic expressions of veneration for the poet's memory; which, she assured me, she felt but in common with the other inhabitants of the village. When we came to the door of the house, we met the peasant, its present possessor. The old woman recommending the stranger and his curiosity, to her neighbour's good offices, departed. I entered immediately, and ran over every room, which the peasant assured me, in confirmation of what I before learnt from better authority, were preserved, as nearly as they could be, in the state Petrarch had left them. The house and premises, having fortunately been transmitted from one enthusiast of his name to another, no tenants have been admitted, but under the strictest prohibition of making any change in the form of the apart-ments, or in the memorial relics belonging to the place: and, to say the truth, every thing I saw in it, save a few articles of the peasant's furniture in the kitchen, has an authentic appearance. Three of the rooms below stairs are particularly shewn, and they have nothing in them but what once belonged to the Poet. In one, which I think they call his parlour, is a very antique cupboard; where, it is supposed, he deposited some precious part of his literary treasure. The ceiling is painted in a grotesque manner. A niche in the wall contains the skeleton of his favourite cat, with a Latin epigram beneath, of Petrarch's composition. It is good enough to deserve being copied; but the lateness of the hour did not allow me time. A little room, beyond this, is said to have been his study: the walls of it, from top to bottom, are scribbled over with sonnets, and poetical eulogies on Petrarch, antient and modern: many of which are subscribed by persons of distinguished rank, and talents, Italians, as well as Strangers. Here, too, is the bard's old chair, and on it is displayed a great deal of heavy, ornamental carpentry; which required no stretch of faith to be believed the manufacture of the fourteenth century. You may be sure, I placed myself in it, with much veneration, and the most resigned assent to Mrs Dobson's relation;* that Petrarch, sitting in this same chair, was found dead in his library, with one arm leaning on a book. Who could sit in Petrarch's chair, void of some effect? I rose not from it without a train of pensive sentiments and soft impressions; which I ever love to indulge. I was now led into a larger room, behind that I first saw; where, it is likely enough, the poet, according to the peasant's information, received the visits of his friends. Its walls were adorned with landscapes and pastoral scenes, in such painting as Petrarch himself might, and is supposed to have executed. Void of taste and elegance, either in the design or colouring, they bear some characteristic marks of the age to which they are, with no improbability, assigned; and, separate from the merit of exhibiting repeatedly the portraits of Petrarch and Laura, are a valuable sketch of the rude infancy of the art, where it rose with such hasty vigour to perfection. Having seen all that was left unchanged, in this consecrated mansion, I passed through a room, said to have been the Bard's bedroom, and stepped into the garden, situated on a green slope, descending directly from the house. It is now rather an orchard,

* Susannah Dobson wrote a *Life of Petrarch* in 1775.

than a garden; a spot of small extent, and without much else to recommend it, but that it was once the property of Petrarch. It is not pretended to have retained the form in which he left it. An agreeably wild and melancholy kind of view, which it commands over the Euganean hills, and which I beheld, under the calm glow of approaching sun-set, must often, at the same moment, have soothed the Poet's anxious feelings, and hushed his active imagination, as it did my own, into a delicious repose. Having lingered here till the sun was sunk beneath the horizon, I was led a little way farther in the village, to see Petrarch's fountain. Hippocrene* itself could not have been more esteemed by the poet, than this, his gift, by all the inhabitants of Arqua. The spring is copious, clear, and of excellent water; I need not say with what relish I drank of it. The last religious act in my little pilgrimage, was a visit to the church-yard; where I strewed a few flowers, the fairest of the season, on the Poet's tomb; and departed for Padua by the light of the moon.

September 7th

Immediately after breakfast, we went to Saint Justina's, a noble temple, designed by Palladio, and worthy of his reputation. The dimensions are vast, and the equal distribution of light and ornament, truly admirable. Upon my first entrance, the long perspective of domes above, and chequered marble below, struck me with surprize and pleasure. I roved about the spacious ailes for several minutes; then sat down under the grand cupola, and admired the beautiful symmetry of the building. Both extremities of the cross ailes are terminated by altars, and tombs of very remote antiquity, adorned with uncouth sculptures of the Evangelists supported by wreathed columns of alabaster; round which, to my no small astonishment, four or five gawky, coarse fellows were waddling on their knees; persuaded, it seems, that this strange devotion would cure the rheumatism or any other aches with which they were afflicted. You can have no conception of the ridiculous attitudes into which they threw themselves; nor the difficulty with which they squeezed along, between the middle column of the tomb, and those which surrounded

*A fountain sacred to the Muses.

it. No criminal in the pillory ever exhibited a more rueful appearance; no swine ever scrubbed itself more fervently than these infatuated lubbers. I left them hard at work; taking more exercise than had been their lot for many a day . . . When we came out of Saint Justina's, the azure of the sky and the softness of the air inclined us to think of some excursion. Where could I wish to go, but to the place in which I had been so delighted? Besides, it was proper to make the C[ornaro family] another visit; and proper to see the Pisani palace, which happily I had before neglected. All these proprieties considered, M. de R[osenberg] accompanied me to Fiesso. The sun was just sunk when we arrived. The whole æther in a glow, and the fragrance of the citron alleys delightful. Beneath them I walked in the cool, till the Galuzzi began once more, her enchanting melody. She sung till the moon tempted the fascinating G[iustiniana – Madame de Rosenberg] and myself to stray on the banks of the Brenta. A profound calm reigned upon the woods and the waters, and moon-light added serenity, to a scene naturally peaceful. We listened to the faint murmurs of the leaves and the distant rural noises, observed the gleams that quivered on the river, and discovered a mutual delight in contemplating the same objects. We supped late: before the Galuzzi had repeated the airs which had most affected me, morning began to dawn.

September 8th

It was evening, and I was still asleep; not in a tranquil slumber, but at the mercy of fantastic visions. The want of sound repose, had thrown me into a feverish, impatient mood, that was alone to be subdued by harmony. Scarcely had I snatched some slight refreshment, before I flew to the great organ at St Justina's, but tried, this time, to compose myself in vain. M. de R. finding my endeavours unsuccessful, proposed, by way of diverting my attention, that we should set out immediately for one of the Euganean hills about six or seven miles from Padua, at the foot of which some antique baths had been very lately discovered. I consented without hesitation, little concerned whither I went, or what happened to me, provided the scene was often shifted. The lanes and inclosures we passed in our road to the hills, appeared in all the gaiety that verdure, flowers, and sunshine could give them. But my pleasures were overcast, and I beheld every object, however chearful, through a dusky medium. Deeply engaged in conversation, distance made no impression; and we beheld the meadow, over which the ruins are scattered, lie before us, when we still imagined ourselves several miles away ... Leaving our carriage at the entrance of the mead, we traversed its flowery surface, and shortly perceived among the grass, an oblong bason, encrusted with pure white marble. Most of the slabs are large and perfect; apparently brought from Greece, and still retaining their polished smoothness. The pipes to convey the waters are still discernible; in short, the whole ground plan may be easily traced. Nothing more remains: the pillars and arcades are fallen; and one or two pedestals alone, vouch for their former existence. Near the principal bath, we remarked the platforms of several circular apartments, paved with mosaic, in a neat, simple taste, far from inelegant. Weeds have not yet sprung up amongst the crevices; and the universal freshness of the ruin shews, that it has not been long exposed ... A profusion of aromatic flowers covered the slopes, and exhaled additional perfumes, as the sun declined, and the still hour approached, which was wont to spread over my mind a divine composure, and to restore the tranquillity, I might have lost in the day. But now, it diffused in vain its reviving coolness; and I remained, if possible, more sad and restless than before ...

September 9th

You may imagine how I felt, when the hour of leaving Padua drew near. It happened to be a high festival, and mass celebrated at the grand church of Saint Anthony, with more than ordinary splendor. The music drawing us thither, we found every chapel twinkling with lights, and the choir filled with a vapour of incense. Through its medium several cloth of gold figures discovered themselves, minis-tring before the altar, and acting their parts with sacred pomposity, wonderfully imposing. I attended very little to their functions; but the plaintive tones of the voices and instruments, so consonant with my own feelings, melted me into tears, and gave me, no doubt, the exterior of exalted piety. Guadagni* sung amongst the other musicians, but seemed to be sinking apace into devotion and obscurity. The ceremony ended, I took leave of M. de R. with sincere regret, and was driven away to Vicenza. Of my journey I scarce know any more, than that the evening was cold and rainy, that I shivered and was miserable.

September 10th

The morning being overcast, I went, full of the spirit of Æschylus, to the Olympic theatre, and vented my evil temper in reciting some of the most tremendous verses of his furies. The august front of the scene and its three grand streets of fanes [temples] and palaces, inspired me with the lofty sentiments of the Grecian drama; but the dubious light, admitted through windows, scarce visible between rows of statues which crown the entablature, sunk me into fits of gloom and sadness. I mused a long while in the darkest and most retired recess of the edifice; fancying I had penetrated into a real and perfect monument of antiquity, which till this moment had remained undiscovered ... After I had given scope to the fancies which the scene suggested, we set out for Verona. The situation is striking and picturesque. A long line of battlement-walls, flanked by venerable towers, mounts the hillside in a grand, irregular sweep, and incloses many a woody garden, and grove of slender cypresses. Beyond, rises an awful assembly of mountains; opposite to which, a fertile plain presents itself, checked with all the variety of meads and thickets, olive-grounds and vineyards. Amongst these our road kept winding, till we entered the city gate, and passed (the post knows how many streets and alleys in the way) to our inn, a lofty, handsome-looking building; but so full, that we were obliged to take up with an apartment on its very summit, open to all the winds, like the magic chamber Apuleius mentions; and commanding the roofs of half Verona. Here and there a pine shot up amongst them, and the shady hills, terminating the perspective with their walls and turrets, formed a romantic scene. Placing our table in a balcony, to enjoy the prospect with greater freedom, we feasted upon fish from the Lago di Garda, and the

* Gaetano Guadagni (*c.* 1725–92), Italian male contralto.

delicious fruits of the country; grapes worthy of Canaan, and peaches, such as Eden itself might have gloried in producing. Thus did I remain, solacing myself; breathing the cool air, and remarking the evening tints of the mountains ... Twilight drawing on, I left my haunt, and, stealing down stairs, enquired for a guide to conduct me to the amphitheatre; perhaps, the most entire monument of Roman days. The people of the house, instead of bringing me a quiet peasant, officiously delivered me up to an antiquary; one of those diligent, plausible young men, to whom, God help me! I have so capital an aversion. This sweet spark displayed all his little erudition, and flourished away upon cloacas and vomitoriums, with eternal fluency. He was very profound in the doctrine of conduits; and knew to admiration, how the filthiness of all the amphitheatre was disposed of: but perceiving my inattention, and having just grace enough to remark, that I chose one side of the street, when he preferred the other; and sometimes trotted, through despair, in the kennel [gutter], he made me a pretty bow, I tipped him half a crown; and, seeing the ruins before me, traversed a gloomy arcade, and emerged alone into the arena. A smooth turf carpets its surface, from which the spacious row of gradines rises to a majestic elevation ... silence reigned undisturbed amongst the awful ruins; nothing moved, save the weeds and grasses which skirt the walls, and tremble with the faintest breeze. I liked the idea of being thus shut in on every side by endless gradines, abandoned to a stillness and solitude I was so peculiarly disposed to taste. Throwing myself upon the grass in the middle of the arena, I enjoyed the freedom of my situation; and pursued the last tracks of light, as they faded behind the solitary arches, which rise above the rest. Red and fatal were the tints of the western sky; the wind blew chill and hollow, and something more than common seemed to issue from the withering herbage on the walls. I started up; and arrived, panting, in the great square before the ruins ...

September 11th

Traversing once more the grand piazza, and casting a last glance upon the amphitheatre, we passed under a lofty arch which terminates the perspective, and left Verona by a wide, airy street, commanding, whenever you look back, a striking scene of towers, cypress, and mountains. The country, between this beautiful town and Mantua, presents one continued grove of dwarfish mulberries, among which start up innumerable barren hills. Now and then a knot of poplars diversify their craggy summits; and, sometimes, a miserable shed. Mantua itself rises out of a morass formed by the Mincio; whose course, in most places, is so choaked up with reeds, as to be scarcely discernible. It requires a creative imagination, to discover any charms at such a prospect; and a strong prepossession, not to be disgusted with the scene where Virgil was born. For my own part, I approached this neighbourhood with proper deference, and began to feel the God; but finding no tufted tree on which I could suspend my lyre, or verdant bank which invited to repose, I abandoned poetry, and entered the city in despair. The beating of drums, and the sight of German whiskers, finished, what croaking frogs and stagnant ditches had begun. Every classic idea being scared by such sounds, and such objects, I dined in dudgeon; and refused stirring out, till late in the evening. A few paces from the town, stand the remains of the palace, where the Gonzagas formerly resided. This, I could not resist looking at; and was amply rewarded. Several of the apartments, adorned by the bold pencil of Julio Romano,* merit the most exact attention . . . When it was too late to examine the paintings any longer, I walked into a sort of court, or rather garden, which had been decorated with fountains and antique statues. Their fragments still remain, amongst beds of weeds and flowers; for every corner of the place is smothered in vegetation. Here, nettles grow thick and rampant; there, tuberoses and jessamine climb around mounds of ruins; which, during the elegant reign of the Gonzagas, led to grottos and subterraneous apartments, concealed from vulgar eyes, and sacred to the most refined enjoyments. I gathered a tuberose, that sprung from a shell of white marble, once trickling with water, now, half filled with mould; and carrying it home, shut myself up for the rest of the night, inhaled its perfume, and fell a dreaming.

* Giulio Romano (c. 1499–1546), Italian painter, architect and engineer.

September 12th

A shower having fallen, the air was refreshed, and the drops still glittered upon the vines, through which our road conducted us. Three or four miles from Mantua, the scene changed to extensive grounds of rice, and meads of the tenderest verdure watered by springs, whose frequent meanders gave to the whole prospect the appearance of a vast green carpet, shot with silver. Further on, we crossed the Po; and, passing Guastalla, entered a woody country, full of inclosures and villages; herds feeding in the meadows, and poultry parading before every wicket. The peasants were busied in winnowing their corn; or, mounted upon the elms and poplars, gathering the rich clusters from the vines that hang streaming in braids from one branch to another. I was surprized to find myself already in the midst of the vintage; and to see every road crouded with carts and baskets, bringing it along: you cannot imagine a pleasanter scene. Round Reggio it grew still more lively; and, on the other side of that agreeable little city, I remarked many a cottage . . . with its garden, and willow hedge in flower, swarming with bees. Our road, the smoothest conceivable, led us, perhaps too rapidly, by so chearful a landscape. I caught glimpses of fields and copses, as we fled along, that could have afforded me amusement for hours; and orchards on gentle acclivities, beneath which, I could have walked till evening. The trees literally bent under their loads of fruit, and innumerable ruddy apples lay scattered upon the ground . . . Beyond these rich masses of foliage, to which the sun lent additional splendor, at the utmost extremity of the pastures, rose the irregular ridge of the Appenines; whose deep blue presented a striking contrast to the glowing colours of the foreground. I fixed my eyes on the chain of distant mountains; and indulged, as usual, my conjectures, of what was going forwards on their summits; of those who tended goats on the edge of the precipice; traversed, at this moment, the dark thickets of pine; and passed their lives in yonder sheds, contented and unknown.* Such were the dreams that filled my fancy, and kept incessantly employed, till it was dusk, and the moon began to show herself; the same moon which, but a few days ago, had seen me so happy at Fiesso. Her soft light reposed upon

* Echoes again of Gray's 'Elegy'.

the meads, that had been newly mown; and the shadows of tall poplars were cast aslant them. I left my carriage; and, running into the dim haze, abandoned myself to the recollection it inspired.* ... At length, having wandered where chance, or the wildness of my fancy led, till the lateness of the evening alarmed me, I regained the chaise as fast as I could, and arrived between ten and eleven at the place of my destination.

Sept. 13th

Having but a moment or two at liberty, I hurried early in the morning to the palace; and entered an elegant Ionic court, with arcades of the whitest stone, through which I caught peeps of a clear blue sky, and groves of cypresses. Some few good paintings still adorn the apartments, but the best part of the collection has been disposed of, for a hundred thousand sequins; amongst which was that inestimable picture, the Notte of Corregio † ... In the other rooms, no picture gave me more pleasure than Jacob's vision, by Domenico Feti.‡ I gazed several minutes at the grand confusion of clouds and seraphim descending around the patriarch; and wished for a similar dream ... Having spent the little time I had remaining in contemplating this object, I hastened from the palace, and left Modena. We traversed a champain country in our way to Bologna, whose richness and fertility encreased, in proportion as we drew near that celebrated mart of lapdogs and sausages ... At present, I thought of very little else, to say truth, but what I had seen at Fiesso; and, what I was to hear at Lucca.§ The anxiety inspired by the one, and impatience by the other, rendered me shamefully insensible to the merit of Bologna; where I passed two hours, and of which I can add nothing, but that it is very much out of humour at this present moment; an earthquake and cardinal Buoncompagni having disarranged both land and people. For half a year, the ground continued trembling; and, for these last months, the legate and senators have grumbled and scratched inces-

* Of Cornaro.

† Antonio Correggio (*c.* 1494–1534), Italian fresco painter, often dealing with mythological subjects.

‡ Domenico Feti (*c.* 1589–1624), painter of mythological and religious subjects.

§ Cornaro at Fiesso and Pacchierotti's singing at Lucca.

santly; so that, between natural and political commotions, the Bolognese must have passed an agreeable summer. Such a report of the situation of things, you may suppose, was not likely to retard my journey: I put off delivering my letters to another opportunity; ran up a tall, slender tower, as high as the Campanile di San Marco, by way of exercise; and proceeded, immediately after dinner toward the mountains. We were soon in the midst of crags, and stony channels, that stream with ten thousand rills in the winter season; but, during the summer months, reflect every sun-beam, and harbour half the scorpions in the country. For many a toilsome league, our prospect consisted of nothing but dreary hillocks, and intervening wastes, more barren and mournful than those to which Mary Magdalene retired. Sometimes a crucifix, or chapel, peeped out of the parched fern and grasses, with which these desolate fields are cloathed; and now and then we met a goggle-eyed pilgrim, trudging along, and staring about him as if he waited only for night and opportunity to have additional reasons for hurrying to Jerusalem. During three or four hours that we continued ascending, the scene increased in sterility and desolation; but, at the end of our second post, the landscape began to alter for the better: little green valleys at the base of the tremendous steeps, discovered themselves; scattered over with oaks, and freshened with running waters, which the nakedness of the impending rocks set off to advantage. The sides of the cliffs in general consist of rude mis-shapen masses; but their summits are smooth and verdant, and continually browsed by herds of white goats, which were gamboling on the edge of precipices, as we passed beneath. I joined one of these frisking assemblies, whose shadows were stretched by the setting sun, along the level herbage. There I sat a few minutes, whilst they shook their beards at me, and tried to scare me with all their horns; but I was not to be frightened, and would offer up my adorations to departing day, in spite of their caperings. Being tired with skipping and butting at me in vain, the whole herd trotted away; and I after them. They led me a rare dance from crag to crag, and from thicket to thicket. It was growing dusky apace, and wreaths of smoke began to ascend from the mysterious depths of valleys. I was ignorant what monster inhabited such retirements, so gave over my pursuit, lest some Polypheme* or other might make me repent it. I looked around, the carriage was out of sight; but hearing the neighing of horses at a distance, I soon came up with them and mounted another rapid ascent; from whence an extensive tract of cliff and forest-land was discernible. The rocks here formed a spacious terrace; along which I continued surveying the distant groves, and marking the solemn approach of night. The sky was hung with storms, and a pale moon seemed to advance with difficulty amongst broken and tempestuous clouds. It was an hour to reap plants with brazen sickles,† and to meditate upon revenge. A chill wind blew from the highest peak of the Appenines, inspiring evil; and making a dismal rustle amongst the woods of chesnuts that hung over the mountain's side, through which we were forced to pass. I never heard such fatal murmurs; nor felt myself so gloomily disposed. I walked out of the sound of the carriage, where the glimmering moon-light prevailed, and began interpreting the language of the leaves, not greatly to my own advantage, or that of any being in the universe. I was no prophet of good but full of melancholy bodings, and something that bordered upon despair. Had I but commanded an oracle, as antient visionaries were wont, I should have thrown whole nations into dismay. How long I continued in this strange temper, I cannot pretend to say, but believe it was midnight before we emerged from the oracular forest, and saw faintly before us the huts of Lognone, where we were to sleep. This blessed hamlet is suspended on the brow of a bleak mountain, and every gust that stirs, shakes the whole village to its foundations. At our approach, two hags stalked forth with lanterns, and invited us with a grin, which I shall always remember, to a dish of mustard and crows gizzards; a dish I was more than half afraid of tasting, lest it should change me to some bird of darkness, condemned to mope eternally on the black rafters of the cottage. After repeated supplications, we procured a few eggs, and some faggots to make a fire. Its blaze gave me courage to hear the hollow blasts, that whistled in the crevices; and, pitching my bed in a

* King of the Cyclops in Sicily.
† A phrase that pleased him and which he continued to use. He had invented it at Coniston in the Lakes the year before.

warm corner, I soon fell asleep; and forgot all my cares and in-
quietudes.

Sept. 14th

The sun had not been long above the horizon, before we set forwards
upon a craggy pavement, hewn out of the rough bosom of cliffs and
precipices. Scarce a tree was visible; and the few that presented
themselves, began already to shed their leaves. The raw nipping air of
the deserts, with difficulty spares a blade of vegetation; and in the
whole range of these extensive eminences, I could not discover a
single cornfield or pasture. Inhabitants, you may guess, there were
none: I would defy even a Scotch highlander to find means of sub-
sistence in so rude a soil. Towards mid-day, we had surmounted the
dreariest part of our journey, and began to perceive a milder landscape. The climate improved, as well as the prospect; and, after a
continual descent of several hours, we saw groves and villages in the
dips of the hills; and met a string of mules and horses laded with
fruit. I purchased some figs and peaches from this little caravan, and,
spreading my repast upon a bank, basked in the sunshine, and gathered
large spikes of lavender in full bloom. Continuing our route, we bid
adieu to the realms of poverty and barrenness, and entered a cultivated
vale, shaded by woody acclivities. Amongst these we wound along –
the peasants singing upon the hills, and driving their cattle to springs
by the road's side; near one of which we dined, in a patriarchal
manner; and, afterwards, pursued our course, through a grove of
taper cypresses, waving with the cool gales of the evening. The heights
were suffused with a ruddy glow, proceeding from the light pink
clouds which floated on the horizon. No others were to be seen. All
nature seemed in a happy, tranquil state; the herds penned in their
folds, and every rustic going to repose. I shared the general calm, for
the first time this many a tedious hour; and traversed the dales in
peace, abandoned to flattering hopes and gay illusions. The full moon
shone propitiously upon me, as I ascended a hill, and discovered
Florence at a distance, surrounded with gardens and terraces, rising
one above another. The serene moon-light on the pale grey tints of
the olive, gave an Elysian, visionary appearance to the landscape. I

never beheld so mild a sky, nor such soft gleams: the mountains were veiled in azure mists, which concealed their rugged summits; and the plains in vapours, that smoothed their irregularities, and diffused a faint aerial hue, to which no description can render justice. I could have contemplated such scenery for hours, and was sorry when I found myself shut up from it, by the gates of Florence. We passed several lofty palaces of the true Tuscan order, with rustic arcades and stout columns, whose solidity and magnificence were not diminished by the shades of midnight. Whilst these grand masses lay dark and solemn, the smooth flag-stone, with which every street is paved, received a chequered gleam, and the Arno, the brightest radiance. Though tired with my jumble over the Appennines, I could not resist the pleasure of walking upon the banks of so celebrated a river, and crossing its bridges; which still echoed with music and conversation. Having gratified the first impulse of curiosity, I returned to Vaninis,* and slept as well as my impatience would allow, till it was time next morning (September 15th) to visit the gallery, and worship the Venus de Medicis. I felt, upon entering this world of taste and elegance, as though I could have taken up my abode in it for ever; but, confused with the multitude of objects, I knew not where to turn myself, and ran childishly by the ample ranks of sculptures; like a butterfly in a parterre, that skims, before it fixes, over ten thousand flowers. Having taken my course down one side of the gallery, I turned the angle and discovered another long perspective, equally stored with prodigies of bronze and marble; paintings on the walls, on the ceilings, in short, everywhere . . . Here are a great many Polemburgs; one, in particular, the strangest I ever beheld. Instead of those soft scenes of woods and waterfalls, he is in general so fond of representing, he has chosen for his subject, Virgil ushering Dante into the regions of eternal punishment, amidst the ruins of flaming edifices, that glare across the infernal waves. These mournful towers harbour innumerable shapes, all busy in preying upon the damned. One capital devil, in the form of an enormous lobster, seems very strenuously employed in mumbling a miserable mortal; who sprawls, though in vain, to escape from his claws. This performance, whimsical as it is, retains all that softness

* Where he was staying.

of tint, and delicacy of pencil, for which Polemburg is renowned. Had not the subject so palpably contradicted the execution, as to become remarkable, I should have passed it over, like a thousand more, and brought you immediately to the Tribune. I dare engage our sensations were similar upon entering this apartment, and beholding such a circle of celestials. Need I say I was enchanted, the moment I set my feet within it, and saw full before me the Venus de Medicis? The warm ivory hue of the original marble, is a beauty no copy has ever imitated; and the softness of the limbs exceeded the liveliest idea I had formed to myself of their perfection. Their symmetry every artist is acquainted with; but do you recollect a faint ruddy cast in the hair; which admirably relieves the whiteness of the forehead? The circumstance, though perhaps accidental, struck me as peculiarly charming: it increased the illusion, and helped me to imagine I beheld a breathing divinity. When I had taken my eyes reluctantly from this beautiful object, I cast them upon a Morpheus of white marble, who lies slumbering at the feet of the goddess, in the form of a graceful child. A dormant lion serves him for a pillow: two ample wings, carved with the utmost delicacy, are gathered under him; two others, budding from his temples, half concealed by a flow of lovely ringlets. His languid hands scarce hold a bunch of poppies; near him creeps a lizard, the companion of his cave. Nothing can be more just than the expression of sleep, in the countenance of the little divinity. His lion too, seems perfectly lulled, and rests his muzzle upon his forepaws, as quiet as a domestic mastiff. I contemplated the God with infinite satisfaction, till I felt an agreeable sleepiness steal over my senses, and should have liked very well to doze away a few hours by his side . . . Sleeping figures, with me, always produce the finest illusion. I easily persuade myself, that I behold the very personage cast into the lethargic state which is meant to be represented; and I can gaze whole hours upon them with complacency. But when I see an archer, in the very act of discharging his arrow; a dancer, with one foot in the air; or a gladiator, extending his fist to all eternity; I grow tired, and ask, when will they perform what they are about? When will the bow twang? the foot come to the ground? or the fist meet its adversary? Such wearisome attitudes I can view with admiration; but never, with pleasure. The wrestlers, for example, in the same apartment, filled me with disgust: I cried out, For heaven's sake! give the throw, and have done ... In my way home, I looked into the cathedral; an enormous fabric, inlaid with the richest marbles, and covered with stars and chequered work, like an old-fashioned cabinet. The architect seems to have turned his building inside out; nothing in art being more ornamented than the exterior, and few churches so simple within ... Not a ray of light reaches this sacred inclosure, but through the medium of narrow windows, high in the dome and richly painted. A sort of yellow tint predominates, which gives additional solemnity to the altar, and paleness to the votary before it. I was sensible of the effect, and obtained at last the colour of sanctity. Having remained some time in this pious hue, I returned home, and feasted upon grapes and ortolans with great edification ...

The following days were to see the intensification of Beckford's friendship with Pacchierotti, the great singer. Yet what should read as a pleasant interlude is marred by Beckford's outrageous selfishness in the way he commandeered the singer, wearing him out with strenuous excursions into the mountains in bad weather. The singer's delicate voice grew hoarse, and he developed a cough to the despair and fury of his fans in Lucca. Pacchierotti himself, who was about forty at the time, seems to have been a gentle and diffident soul. Tall and thin, awkward in movement and plain of face, he was nevertheless considered by Dr Burney to be the greatest singer he had ever heard. Whole orchestras had been known to break down in tears at the pathos of his singing which, according to Lord Mount Edgecumbe, was 'an extensive soprano, full and sweet in the highest degree'. Though his technique was superb, Pacchierotti had far too much taste and good sense to show off, Lord Mount Edgecumbe tells us, reserving his pyrotechnics for one aria and 'agilita' in each opera, knowing 'that the chief delight of singing and his own excellence lay in touching expression and exquisite pathos'.[9] This the Marchioness Solari also comments upon, describing Pacchierotti's excessive sensibility, and how his 'metaphysical powers often got the better of his physical, something corroborated by the man himself. '*I sang very devoutly indeed to obtain a quiet for his soul*,' [10] *he told Dr Burney when he sang at Galuppi's funeral mass.*

The opera currently playing at Lucca and in which Beckford so greatly admired him was Bertoni's Quinto Fabio.

Friday, September 16th

My impatience to hear Pacchierotti, called me up with the sun. I blessed a day which was to give me the greatest of musical pleasures, and travelled gayly towards Lucca, along a fertile plain, bounded by rocky hills, and scattered over with towns and villages. We passed Pistoia in haste, and, about three in the afternoon, entered the Lucchese territory, by a clean paved road, which runs through some of the pleasantest copses imaginable, bordered with variety of heaths and broom, in blossom. Sometimes it conducted us down slopes, overgrown with shrubby chesnuts and arbor vitæ; sometimes, between groves of cypress and pines laden with cones: a red soil peeping forth from the vegetation, adds to the richness of the landscape, which swells, all the way, into gentle acclivities; and, round the town, spreads into mountains, green to their very summits, and diversified with gardens and palaces. A more pleasing scenery can with difficulty be imagined. I was quite charmed with beholding it, as I knew very well the opera would keep me a long while, chained down in its neighbourhood. Happy for me, that the environs of Lucca were so beautiful; since I defy almost any city to contain more ugliness within its walls. Narrow streets and dismal alleys; wide gutters and cracked pavements; everybody in black, like mourners for the gloom of their habitations, which however are large and lofty enough for conscience; but, having all grated windows, they convey none but dark, and dungeon-like ideas. My spirits fell many degrees upon entering this sable capital; and when I found Friday was meagre day, in every sense of the word, with its inhabitants, and no opera to be performed, I grew terribly out of humour, and shut myself up in a chamber of the inn; which, to compleat my misfortune, was crowded with human lumber. Instead of a delightful symphony, I heard nothing for some time but the clatter of plates and the swearing of waiters. Amongst the number of my tormentors was a whole Genoese family of distinction; very fat and sleek, and terribly addicted to the violin. Hearing of my fondness for music, they speedily got together a few scrapers, and began such an academia, as drove me to one end of the room, whilst they possessed the other. The hopes and heir of the family, a coarse chubby dolt of about eighteen, played out of all time, and, during the intervals of repose he gave his elbow, burst out into a torrent of common-place, which compleated, you may imagine, my felicity. Pacchierotti, whom they all worshipped in their heavy way, sat silent the while in a corner; the second Soprano warbled, not absolutely ill, at the harpsichord; whilst the old lady, young lady, and attendant females, kept ogling him with great perseverance. Those who could not get in, squinted through the crevices of the door. Abbés and greyhounds were fidgetting continually about. In short, I was so worried, that, pleading head-aches and lassitudes, I escaped about ten o'clock, and shook myself, when I got safe to my apartment, like a spaniel just fresh from a dripping copse.

Lucca, September 25th

You ask how I pass my time. Generally upon the hills, in wild spots where the arbutus flourishes; from whence I may catch a glimpse of the distant sea; my horse tied to a cypress, and myself cast upon the grass, like Palmarin of Oliva,* with a tablet and pencil in my hand, a basket of grapes by my side, and a crooked stick to shake down the chesnuts. I have bidden adieu, several days ago, to the dinners and glories of the town, to visits and conversationes, and only come thither in an evening, just time enough for the grand march which precedes Pacchierotti in *Quinto Fabio*. Sometimes he accompanies me in my excursions, to the utter discontent of the Lucchese, who swear I shall ruin their opera, by leading him such confounded rambles amongst the mountains, and exposing him to the inclemency of winds and showers. One day, they made a vehement remonstrance, but in vain; for the next, away we trotted over hill and dale, and stayed so late in the evening, that cold and hoarseness were the consequence. The

* An emperor in a sixteenth-century chivalric romance by Francisco de Moraes.

whole republic was thrown into a commotion, and some of its prime ministers deputed to harangue Pacchierotti, upon the rides he had committed. Billingsgate never produced such furious orators. Had the safety of their mighty state depended upon this imprudent excursion, they could not have vociferated with greater violence. You know I am rather energetic, and, to say truth, I had very near got into a scrape of importance, and drawn down the execrations of the Gonfalonier and all his council upon my head, in defending him, and in openly declaring our intention of taking, next morning, another ride over the rocks, and absolutely losing ourselves in the clouds, which veil their acclivities. These threats were put into execution, and, yesterday, we made a tour of about thirty miles upon the high lands, and visited a variety of castles and palaces. The Conte Nobili conducted us, a noble Lucchese, but born in Flanders, and educated at Paris. He possess the greatest elegance of imagination, and a degree of sensibility, rarely met with upon our gross planet. The way did not appear tedious in such company. The sun was tempered by light clouds, and a soft autumnal haze rested upon the hills, covered with shrubs and olives. The distant plains and forests appeared tinted with deep blue; and I am now convinced the azure so prevalent in Velvet Breughel's landscapes,* is not exaggerated. After riding for six or seven miles along the cultivated levels, we began to ascend a rough slope, overgrown with chesnuts; here and there, some vines streaming in garlands displayed their clusters. A great many loose fragments and stumps of antient pomegranates perplexed our route; which continued, turning and winding through this sort of wilderness, till it opened on a sudden to the side of a lofty mountain covered with tufted groves; amongst which hangs the princely castle of the Garzonis, on the very side of a precipice. Alcina † could not have chosen a more romantic situation. The garden lies extended beneath, gay with flowers, and glittering with compartments of spar; which, though in no great purity of taste, has an enchanted effect, for the first time.

* Jan Breughel (1568–1625). Younger son of Pieter Breughel the Elder, and brother of the 'Hell-fire' Breughel mentioned on p. 29. Known as 'Velvet' for his small-scale landscapes and still-lifes.
† The witch in *Orlando Innamorato* and *Orlando Furioso*. See note on p. 36.

Two large marble basons, with jet d'eaux seventy feet in height, divide the parterres; from the extremity of which rises a rude cliff, shaded with firs and ilex, and cut into terraces. Leaving our horses at the great gate of this magic inclosure, we passed through the spray of the fountains, and, mounting an almost endless flight of steps, entered an alley of oranges, and gathered ripe fruit from the trees. Whilst we were thus employed, the sun broke from the clouds, and lighted up the vivid greens of the vegetation; at the same time spangling the waters, which pour copiously down a succession of rocky terraces, and sprinkle the impending citron-trees with perpetual dew. These streams issue from a chasm in the cliff, surrounded by cypresses, which conceal, by their thick branches, some pavilions with baths. Above rises a colossal statue of Fame, boldly carved, and in the very act of starting from the precipices. A narrow path leads up to the feet of the goddess, on which I reclined; whilst a vast column of water arched over my head, and fell, without even wetting me with its spray, into the depths below. I could with difficulty prevail upon myself to abandon this cool recess, which the fragrance of bay and orange, extracted by constant showers, rendered uncommonly luxurious. At last, I consented to move on, through a dark walk of ilex, which, to the credit of Signior Garzoni be it spoken, is suffered to grow as wild, and as forest-like, as it pleases. This grove is suspended on the mountain side, whose summit it cloathed with a boundless wood of olives, and forms by its azure colour, a striking contrast with the deep verdure of its base. After resting a few moments in the shade, we proceeded to a long avenue (bordered by aloes in bloom, forming majestic pyramids of flowers thirty feet high) which led us to the palace. This was soon run over. Then, mounting our horses, we wound amongst sunny vales, and inclosures with myrtle hedges, till we came to a rapid steep. We felt the heat most powerfully in ascending it, and were glad to take refuge under a bower of vines, which continues for miles along its summit, almost without interruption. These arbours afforded us both shade and refreshment: I fell upon the clusters, which formed our ceiling, like a native of the north, unused to such luxuriance; like one of those Goths, which Gray so poetically describes, who

Scent the new fragrance of the breathing rose,
*And quaff the pendant vintage as it grows.**

I wish you had journeyed with us under this fruitful canopy, and observed the partial sunshine through its transparent leaves, and the glimpses of blue sky, it every now and then admitted. I say only, every now and then; for, in most places, a sort of verdant gloom prevailed, exquisitely agreeable in so hot a day. But such luxury did not last, you may suppose, for ever. We were soon forced from our covert, and obliged to traverse a mountain, exposed to the sun, which had dispersed every cloud, and shone with intolerable brightness. On the other side of this extensive eminence, lies an agreeable hillock, surrounded by others, woody and irregular. Wide vineyards and fences of Indian corn lay between, across which the Conte Nobili conducted us to his house, where we found a very comfortable dinner prepared. We drank the growth of the spot, and defied Constantia and the Cape to exceed it. Afterwards, retiring into a wood of the Marchese Mansi, with neat pebble walks and trickling rivulets, we sipped coffee, and loitered till sun-set. It was then time to return: the dews began to fall, and the mists to rise from the valleys. The profound calm and silence of evening, threw us all three into our reveries. We went pacing along heedlessly, just as our horses pleased, without hearing any sound but their steps. Between nine and ten we entered the gates of Lucca. Pacchierotti coughed, and half its inhabitants wished us at the devil. I think now I have detained you long enough with my excursions; you must require a little repose; for my own part, I am heartily tired. I intended to say some things about certain owls, amongst other grievances, I am pestered with in this republic; but shall cut them all short, and wish you good night; for the opera is already begun, and I would not miss the first, glorious recitative for the empire of Trebizond.

Music stirred strange fires in him. The day before leaving Lucca, he wrote apropos to Cozens: 'I care not a grain of millet whether my name be engraven on marble or graces the annals of a kingdom, not I.

* Thomas Gray, *The Alliance of Education and Government.*

Give me but a secure retirement with those I love, surround me with impervious forests and keep off the world: keep off Ministers, Generals, Senators, Sportsmen, Courtiers, pendants, and Sectaries. Give me ignorance and tranquillity, those may take science and labour that chuse ... If ever you see ambition beginning to fire my bosom,' he went on, 'quench the flame and continually repeat that it is better to be meanly happy than illustriously miserable. I have never greater need to be reminded of this belief, than during some moments of Pacchierotti's declamation, which breathes such exalted heroism, that forgetting my peaceful schemes I start up, grow restless, stride about and begin to form ambitious projects. Musick raises before me a host of phantoms which I pursue with eagerness, my blood thrills in my veins, its whole current is changed and agitated, I can no longer command myself and whilst the frenzy lasts, would willingly be devoted to destruction. These are perilous emotions and would lead me cruelly away.' [11]

The music, or rather the singing, which so unhinged Beckford and which, in his own words, also made him 'more than ever effeminate', will never be heard again. This was the singing of the castrati, the musici, who dominated Italian opera throughout the eighteenth century. It was said indeed that seventy per cent of all male opera singers at the time were eunuchs, since women, especially at Rome and Naples, were forbidden to take the stage for fear that they would inflame the uncertain passions of the audience and cause bloodshed.

'Their voices have always something dry and harsh,' wrote de Brosses of the castrati, 'quite different from the youthful softness of women, but they are brilliant, light, full of sparkle, very loud and with a very wide range.' [12] It seems to have been a sound that at first repelled then grew upon the ear, though there were English visitors to Italy who couldn't endure the 'shake' the castrati affected, let alone the unhappy process that had rendered them capable of such singing.

Making his inquiries through a web of secrecy and evasion, Dr Burney discovered that the castrati were usually, though not always, children of poor parents, coming mainly from Apulia, or from the country round the small town of Norcia on the Marches. Any child with a promising voice was considered an investment by his parents, who would take him to the conservatoires in the big cities for a voice test, *after which the unfortunate boy underwent the operation that was legally forbidden on pain of death, but to which the authorities turned a blind eye. The surgeons of Bologna were considered experts in the matter, though the traveller M. de la Lande had discovered shops in Naples advertising* 'Qui si castrano ragazzi' – *Boys castrated. D'Ancillon in his* Traité des eunuques *evokes nightmarishly the operation, how* 'the child, often drugged with opium or some other narcotic, was placed in a very hot bath, until it was in a state of virtual insensibility. Then the ducts leading to the testicles were severed, so that the latter in course of time shrivelled and disappeared.'[13] *It was commonly thought at the time that the later the boy was castrated the lower his voice would be, but it seems more likely that those who would have naturally grown into tenors became male sopranos, and baritones, contraltos. Dr Burney discovered that the boys, though subject to a strict educational regime, were well looked after in order to safeguard their delicate voices, though there were cases of many in the Neapolitan conservatoire who ran away.*

In their time the castrati *were regarded with the adulation now accorded to pop-stars, and both men and women so frequently fell in love with them that they were considered to be arch-corrupters of morals.* '... His breast was in no way inferior, either in form or in beauty, to any woman's,' *writes Casanova of Cardinal Borghese's favourite singer,* 'and it was above all by this means that the monster made such ravages. Though one knew the negative nature of this unfortunate,' *Casanova continues,* 'curiosity made one glance at his chest, and an inexpressible charm acted upon one, so that you were madly in love before you realized it.'[14]

Many of the castrati *grew grossly spoilt in consequence, manipulating the orchestras to suit their own private style, and when not singing, openly striding about taking snuff and talking to members of the cast or audience. But the greatest of them lived like princes, and there were many among them who lived dedicated and noble lives. Their decline came towards the end of the century with the popularity of the more chaste and simple music of Gluck, and vanished altogether under the Europe of Napoleon. The use of the* castrati *in Church music, however, persisted into the nineteenth century, Moreschi, the*

last of them, performing before Victor Emmanuel II and Umberto I,
and dying in 1922.

Livorno, October 2d

No sooner were we beyond the gates, than we found ourselves in
narrow roads, shut in by vines and grassy banks of canes and oziers,
rising high above our carriage, and waving their leaves in the air.
Through the openings, which sometimes intervene, we discovered a
variety of hillocks, cloathed with shrubberies and verdure; ruined
towers looking out of the bushes: not one without a romantic tale
attending it. This sort of scenery lasted till, passing the baths, we
beheld Pisa, rising from an extensive plain, the most open we had as
yet seen in Italy, crossed by an aqueduct. We were set down immediately before the Duomo, which stands insulated in a verdant opening,
and is by far the most curious and highly-finished edifice my eyes
ever viewed. Don't ask what shape, or architecture; it is almost impossible to tell, so great is the confusion of ornaments. The capitals
of the columns and carving of the architraves, as well as the form of
the arches, are evidently of Grecian design, but Gothic proportions.
The dome gives the mass an oriental appearance, which helped to
bewilder me; in short, I have dreamt of such buildings, but little
thought they existed. On one side you survey the famous tower, as
perfectly awry as I expected; on the other the baptistery, a circular
edifice, distinct from the church, and right opposite its principal
entrance; crouded with sculptures, and topped by the strangest of
cupolas . . . Our next object was the Campo Santo, which forms one
side of the opening in which the cathedral is situated. The walls, and
gothic tabernacle above the entrance, rising from a level turf, appear
as fresh, as if built within the century, and, preserving a neat straw-
colour, have the cleanliest effect imaginable. Our guide unlocking the
gates, we entered a spacious cloister, forming an oblong quadrangle,
inclosing the sacred earth of Jerusalem, conveyed thither about the
period of the crusades, in the days of Pisanese prosperity. The holy
mould produces a rampant crop of weeds; but none are permitted to
spring from the pavement, which is entirely composed of tombs with
slabs and monumental inscriptions, smoothly laid. Ranges of slender

pillars, formed of the whitest marble and glistening in the sun, support the arcades, which are carved with innumerable stars and roses, partly gothic, and partly saracenial ... I was quite seized by the strangeness of the place, and paced fifty times round and round the cloisters, discovering at every time, some odd novelty. When tired, I seated myself on a fair slab of *giallo antico*, that looked a little cleaner than its neighbours, (which I only mention to identify the precise point of view) and looking through the fillagreed covering of the arches, observed the domes of the cathedral, cupola of the baptistery, and roof of the leaning tower, rising above the leads, and forming the strangest assemblage of pinnacles, perhaps, in Europe. The place is neither sad, nor solemn; the arches are airy; the pillars light; and there is so much caprice, such an exotic look in the whole scene, that, without any violent effort of imagination, one might imagine oneself in fairy land ... It was between ten and eleven when we entered the Campo Santo, and one o'clock struck, before I could be persuaded to leave it; and 'twas the sun which then drove me away; whose heat was so powerful, that all the inhabitants of Pisa shewed their wisdom, by keeping within doors. Not an animal appeared in the streets, except five camels laden with water, stalking along a range of garden walls, and pompous mansions, with an awning before every door. We were obliged to follow their steps, at least, a quarter of a mile, before we reached our inn. Ice was the first thing I sought after, and when I had swallowed an unreasonable portion, I began not to think quite so much of the deserts of Africa, as the heat and the camels had induced me, a moment ago. Early in the afternoon, we proceeded to Livourno, through a wild tract of forest, somewhat in the style of our English parks. The trees, in some places, formed such shady arbours, that we could not resist the desire of walking beneath them and were well rewarded; for after struggling through a rough thicket, we entered a lawn, hemmed in by oaks and chesnuts, which extends several leagues along the coast, and conceals the prospect of the ocean; but we heard its murmur. Nothing could be smoother or more verdant, than the herbage, which was sprinkled with daisies and purple crocuses, as in the month of May. I felt all the genial sensations of spring steal into my bosom, and was greatly delighted upon discovering vast bushes of myrtle, in bloom. The softness of the air, the sound of the distant surges, the evening gleams, and the repose of the landscape, quieted the tumult of my spirits; and I experienced the calm of my instant hours. I lay down in the open turf-walks between the shrubberies; listlessly surveyed the cattle browsing at a distance, and the blue hills, that rose above the foliage and bounded the view. During a few moments I had forgotton every care; but when I began to enquire into my happiness, I found it vanish. I felt myself without those I love most, in situations they would have warmly admired; and, without them, these pleasant meads and woodlands were of little avail. On the contrary, they reminded me so strongly of their absence, that my joy was changed into tears. I looked earnestly at the distant hills, and sighed: I scattered the blossoms I had gathered, and cried out incessantly, Let us drive away. We had not left this woody region far behind, when the Fanalé* began to lift itself above the horizon; the Fanalé you have so often mentioned: the sky and the ocean glowing with amber light, and the ships out at sea, appearing in a golden haze, of which we have no conception in our northern climates. Such a prospect, together with the fresh gales from the Mediterranean, charmed me: I hurried immediately to the port, and sat on a reef of rocks, listening to the waves, that broke amongst them.

October 3d

I went, as you would have done, to walk on the mole as soon as the sun began to shine upon it. Its construction you are no stranger to; therefore I think I may spare myself the trouble of saying more about it, except that the port which it embraces is no longer crouded. Instead of ten ranks of vessels, there are only three; and those consist chiefly of Corsican galleys, that look as poor and tattered as their masters. Not much attention did I bestow upon such objects; but, taking my seat at the extremity of the quay, surveyed the smooth plains of ocean, the coast scattered over with watch-towers, and the rocky isle of Gorgona, emerging from the morning mists, which still lingered upon the horizon. Whilst I was musing upon the scene, and calling up all that train of ideas before my imagination, which possessed your own upon beholding it, an antient figure, with a beard that would have suited a sea-god, stepped out of a boat, and, tottering

* A tower at Livorno, perhaps the Torre del Marzocco, built in 1423.

up the steps of the quay, presented himself before me, with a basket in his hand. He staid dripping a few moments before he pronounced a syllable, and when he began his discourse, I was in doubt, whether I should not have moved off in a hurry: there was something so wan and singular in his countenance. Except this being, no other was visible, for a quarter of a mile at least. I knew not what strange adventure I might be upon the point of commencing; or what message I was to expect from the submarine divinities. However, after all my conjectures, the figure turned out to be no other than an old fisherman, who, having picked up a few large branches of red coral, offered them for sale. I eagerly made the purchase, and thought myself a favourite of Neptune; since he allowed me to acquire, for next to nothing, some of his most beautiful ornaments. My bargain thus expeditiously finished, I ran along the quay with my basket of coral, and, jumping into a boat, was rowed back to the gate of the port. The carriage waited there: I filled it with jasmine, shut myself up in the shade of green blinds, and was driven away at a rate that favoured my impatience. We bowled smoothly over the lawns, I attempted to describe in my last letter, amongst myrtles in flower, that would have done honour to Juan Fernandes.* Arrived at Pisa, I scarcely allowed myself a moment to revisit the Campo Santo; but, after taking my usual portion of ice and pomegranate-seeds, hurried on to Lucca as fast as the horses could carry me, threw the whole idle town into a stare by my speedy return, and gave myself up to *Q. Fabio*.

Next day (October 4th) was passed in running over my old haunts upon the hills, and bidding farewell to several venerable chesnuts, for which I had contracted a sort of friendship, by often experiencing their protection. I could not help feeling some melancholy sensations, when I turned round, the last time, to bid them adieu. Who knows but some dryad, inclosed within them, was conscious of my gratitude, and noted them down on the bark of her tree? It was late before I finished my excursion, and soon after I had walked as usual upon the ramparts, the opera began.

* The island, off the coast of Chile, on which Alexander Selkirk, the model for Robinson Crusoe, was marooned.

Florence, October 5th

It was not without regret, that I forced myself from Lucca. We had all the same road to go over again that brought us to this important republic, but we broke down by way of variety. The wind was chill, the atmosphere damp, and clogged with unwholsome vapours, through which we were forced to walk for a league, whilst our chaise lagged after us. Taking shelter in a miserable cottage, we remained shivering and shaking, till the carriage was in some sort of order, and then proceeded so slowly, that we did not arrive at Florence till late in the evening. We found an apartment over the Arno prepared for our reception. The river, swollen with rains, roared like a mountain torrent. Throwing open my windows, I viewed its agitated course by the light of the moon, half concealed in stormy clouds, which hung above the fortress of Belvedere, and cast a lowering gleam over the hills, which rise above the town, and wave with cypress. I sat contemplating the effect of the shadows on the bridge, on the heights of Boboli, and and the mountain covered with pale olive-groves, amongst which a convent is situated, till the moon sunk into the blackest quarter of the sky, and a bell began to toll. Its sullen sound filled me with sadness; I closed the casements, called for lights, ran to a harpsichord Vannini had prepared for me, and played somewhat in the strain of Jomelli's *Miserere.

October 6th

Every cloud was dispersed when I arose; the sunbeams flittered on the stream, and the purity and transparence of the æther, added new charms to the woody eminences around. Such was the clearness of the air, that even objects on the distant mountains were distinguishable. I felt quite revived by this exhilarating prospect, and walked in the splendor of sunshine to the porticos beneath the famous gallery, then to an antient castle, raised in the days of the republic, which fronts the grand piazza. Colossal statues and venerable terms are placed before it. On one side a fountain clung around with antic figures of bronze, by John of Bologna,† so admirably wrought as to

* Niccolò Jommelli (1714-74), Neapolitan composer of operas.
† John of Bologna (Giambologna) (1529-1608), the most famous Florentine sculptor after Michelangelo.

hold me several minutes in astonishment. On the other, three lofty gothic arches, and, under one of them, the Perseus of Benvenuto Cellini* raised on a pedestal, incomparably designed and executed; which I could not behold uninterested, since its author has ever occupied a distinguished place in my kalendar of genius . . . I dined in peace and solitude, read over your letters, and repaired as evening drew on, to the thickets of Boboli. What a serene sky! What mellowness in the tints of the mountains! A purple haze concealed the bases, whilst their summits were invested with saffron light, discovering every white cot, and every copse, that cloathed their declivities. The prospect widened as I ascended the terraces of the garden. After traversing many long alleys, brown with impending foliage, I emerged into a green opening on the brow of the hill, and seated myself under the statue of Ceres. From this high point I surveyed the mosaic cupolas of the Duomo, its quaint turret, and one still more grotesque in its neighbourhood, built not improbably in the style of antient Etruria. Beyond this singular group of buildings, a plain stretches itself far and wide, scattered over with villas, gardens, and groves of pine and olive, quite to the feet of the mountains. After I had marked the sun's going down, I went, through a plat of vines hanging on the steeps, to a little eminence, round which the wood grows wilder and more luxuriant, and the cypresses shoot up to a surprising elevation. The pruners have spared this sylvan corner, and suffered the bays to put forth their branches, and the ilex to dangle over the walks, many of whose entrances are nearly over grown. I enjoyed the gloom of these shady arbours, in the midst of which rises a lofty pavilion with galleries running round it, not unlike the idea one forms of Turkish chiosks. Beneath, like a garden of vines and rose trees, which I visited, and found a spring under a rustic arch of grotto-work fringed round with ivy. Millions of fish inhabit here, of that beautiful glittering species which comes from China. This golden nation were leaping after insects, as I stood gazing upon the deep clear water, and listening to the drops that trickle from the cove. Opposite to which, at the end of an alley of vines, you discover an oval bason, and, in the midst of it, a statue of Ganymede, sitting

* Benvenuto Cellini (1500–71), Florentine sculptor and goldsmith.

reclined upon the eagle, full of that graceful languor so peculiarly Grecian. Whilst I was musing on the margin of the spring (for I returned to it after casting a look upon the sculpture) the moon rose above the tufted foliage of the terraces. Her silver brightness was strongly contrasted by the deep green of the holm-oak and bay, amongst which I descended by several flights of stairs, with neat marble ballustrades crowned by vases of aloes. It was about seven o'clock, and everybody was jumbling to my Lord T(ylney)'s,* who lives in a fine house, all over blue and silver, with stuffed birds, alabaster cupids, and a thousand prettinesses more: but, after all, neither he nor his abode are worth mentioning. I found a deal of slopping and sipping of tea going forwards, and many dawdlers assembled. As I can say little good of the party, I had better shut the door, and conduct you to the opera, which is really a striking spectacle. However, it being addressed to the sight alone, I was soon tired, and gave myself up to conversation. Bedini, first Soprano, put my patience to severe proof, during the few minutes I attended. You never beheld such a porpoise. If these animals were to sing, I should conjecture it would be in his style. You may suppose how often I invoked Pacchier-otti, and regretted the lofty melody of *Quinto Fabio*. Every body seemed as well contented as if there were no such thing as good music in the world, except a Neapolitan Duchess, who delighted me by her vivacity. We took our fill of maledictions, and went home equally pleased with each other, for having mutually execrated both singers and audience. This, you will say, is not infinitely to our advantage. That I allow; but, tell you truth I must, whether I will or not. Some daemon, envious of your having too favourable an opinion of me, forces me every now and then to confessions, which ought to go great lengths to destroy it. Least, therefore, I should transgress all bounds during this communicative moment, and disclose adventures, sacred as the mysteries of Eleusis,† I had better fold up my letter, and assure you abruptly of my remaining ever, your affectionate, etc. etc.

*

* John Tylney, Earl of Castlemaine (1712–84), a notorious homosexual 'who left his country for his country's sake'!
† Rites held in honour of Demeter.

He was currently engaging in a ripely self-indulgent correspondence with Madame de Rosenberg's friend, Count Benincasa. The subject, of course, was his affair with Cornaro. How he regretted leaving Venice, though perhaps, on his return towards the end of the year, he might yet once again renew the strange passion. Nothing could soothe him. Pacchierotti at Lucca had done what he could, but to no avail; his torments were ever with him. 'One image alone possesses me,' he wrote the Count on the 21st of October from Florence. 'Write to me without fail at Rome, I beg of you, and after that at Naples, where I shall be nursing my sorrows for a month.' [15]

October 22d

They say the air is worse this year at Rome than ever, and that it would be madness to go thither during its malign influence. This was very bad news indeed, to one heartily tired of Florence; at least of its society. Merciful Powers! what a set harbour within its walls!* You may imagine, I do not take vast, or vehement delight in this company, though very ingenious, praise-worthy, and etc. The woods of the Cascini shelter me every morning; and there grows an old crooked ilex at their entrance, twisting round a pine, upon whose branches I sit for hours; hear, without feeling, the showers trickling above my head, and see the cattle browsing peacefully in their pastures, which hazle copses, Italian pines, and groves of cypress inclose. In the afternoon, I never fail hiding myself in the thickets of Boboli, and marking the golden glow of sun-set between their leaves. The other evening I varied my walks, and ascended one of those pleasant hills which rise in the vicinity of the city, and commands a variegated scene of spires, towns, villas, cots, and gardens. On the right, as you stand upon the brow, appears Fesule, with its turrets and white houses, covering a rocky mount; to the left, the vast Val d'Arno, lost in immensity . . . I staid till sun-set, and then, stretching myself out at length upon the level green which forms the summit of the hill, looked down upon the plains below, between the cypresses, and marked the awful waving of their boughs. Next day, a very opposite

---

* It consisted, Beckford notes in the margin of his book, of 'Lord and Lady Cowper, old Ld. Orford, Ld. Tilney, Mr Chace, Mr Patch . . .'

scene engaged me, though much against my will. Her R.H. the G. Duchess having produced a princess in the night, every body put on grand gala in the morning; and I was carried along with the glittering tide of courtiers, ministers, and ladies, to see the christening. After hearing the Grand Duke talk politics for some time, the doors of a temporary chapel were thrown open. Trumpets flourished, processions marched, and the archbishop began his business, at an altar of massive gold, placed under a yellow silk pavilion, with pyramids of lights before it. Wax tapers, though it was noon-day, shone in every corner of the apartments. Two rows of pages, gorgeously accoutered, and holding enormous torches, stood on each side his Royal Highness, and made him the prettiest courtesies imaginable, to the sound of an execrable band of music, though led by Nardini.* The poor old archbishop, who looked very piteous and saint-like, struck up the Te Deum with a quavering voice, and the rest followed him full gallop. That ceremony being despatched (for his R.H. was in a mighty fidget to shrink back into his beloved obscurity) the crowd dispersed, and I went, with a few others, to dine at my Lord Tylney's. Evening drawing on, I ran to throw myself into the woods of Boboli, and remained till it was night, in their profound recesses. Really, this garden is enough to bewilder an enthusiastic spirit; there is something so solemn in its shades, its avenues, and spires of cypresses. When I had mused for many a melancholy hour amongst them, I emerged into the orangery before the palace, which overlooks the largest district of the town, and beheld, as I slowly descended the road which leads up to it, certain bright lights glancing across the cupola of the Duomo and the points of the highest towers. At first I thought them meteors, or those illusive fires which often dance before the eye of my imagination; but soon I was convinced of their reality; for in a few minutes the battlements of the old castle, which I remember mentioning in a former letter, shone with lamps; the lantern of the cathedral was lighted up on a sudden; whilst a stream of torches ran along its fantastic turrets. I enjoyed this prospect at a distance: when near, its pleasures greatly diminished, for half the fish in the town were frying to rejoice the hearts of H.R. Highness's loyal subjects, and

* Pietro Nardini (1722-93), violinist and composer.

bonfires blazing in every street and alley. Hubbubs and stinks of every denomination, drove me quickly to the theatre; but that was all glitter and glare. No taste, no arrangement; paltry looking-glasses, and rat's-tail candles. I had half a mind to return to Boboli.

October 23rd

Do you recollect our evening rambles last year, upon the hill of pines; and the dark valley, where we used to muse in the twilight? I remember, we often fancied the scene like Valombrosa; and vowed, if ever an occasion offered, to visit that deep retirement. I had put off the execution of this pilgrimage from day to day, till the warm weather was gone; and the Florentines declared, I should be frozen if I attempted it. Everybody stared, last night at the opera, when I told them, I was going to bury myself in fallen leaves, and hear no music but their rustlings. Mr Lettice was just as eager as myself to escape the chit-chat and nothingness of Florence:* so we finally determined upon our expedition; and mounting our horses, set out this morning; happily without any company, but the spirit which led us along. We had need of inspiration, since nothing else, I think, would have tempted us over such dreary, uninteresting hillocks, as rise from the banks of the Arno. The hoary olive is their only vegetation; so that nature, in this country, seems in a withering decrepit state; and may not unaptly be compared to 'an old woman clothed in grey'. However, we did not suffer the prospect to damp our enthusiasm, which was the better preserved for Valombrosa. About half way, our palfreys thought proper to look out for some oats; and I, to creep into a sort of granary in the midst of a barren waste, scattered over with white rocks, that reflected more heat than I cared for; although I had been told, snow and ice were to be my portion. Seating myself on the floor between heaps of corn, I reached down a few purple clusters of muscadine grapes, which hung to dry in the ceiling; and amused myself very pleasantly with them till the horses had finished their

* Mr Lettice seems to have been frequently complaisant: 'I should like to lead a Life of three Moons amongst the Lakes,' he had cried the year before, when Beckford had said how much he should like to live a wild and savage life there fishing for sustenance! (1799 Pocket-book, Coniston. Hamilton Papers.)

meal, and it was lawful to set forwards. We met with nothing but rocky steeps, shattered into fragments, and such roads as half inclined us to repent our undertaking; but cold was not yet amongst the number of our evils. At last, after ascending a tedious while, we began to feel the wind blow sharp from the peaks of the mountains; and to hear the murmur of the forests of pine, which shade their acclivities. A paved path leads across them, quite darkened by boughs, which meeting over our heads cast a gloom and a chill below, that would have stopped the proceedings of reasonable mortals, and sent them back to bask in the plain; but, being not so easily discomfited, we threw ourselves boldly into the grove. It presented one of those confusions of tall straight stems I am so fond of; and exhaled a fresh aromatic odour, that revived my spirits. The cold to be sure was piercing; but, setting that at defiance, we galloped on, and issued shortly into a vast amphitheatre of lawns and meadows, surrounded by thick woods beautifully green. Flocks of sheep were dispersed on the slopes, whose smoothness and verdure equal our English pastures. Steep cliffs, and mountains, cloathed with beech to their very summits, guard this retired valley. The herbage, moistened by streams which fall from the eminences, has never been known to fade; and, whilst the chief part of Tuscany is parched by the heats of summer, these upland meadows retain the freshness of spring. I regretted not having visited them sooner, as autumn had, already, made great havock amongst the foliage. Showers of leaves blew full in our faces, as we rode towards the convent, placed at an extremity of the vale, and sheltered by remote firs and chesnuts, towering one above another. Alighting before the entrance, two fathers came out, and received us into the peace of their retirement. We found a blazing fire, and tables spread very comfortably before it, round which five or six over-grown friars were lounging, who seemed, by the sleekness and rosy hue of their countenances, not totally to have despised this mortal existence. My letters of recommendations soon brought the heads of the order about me, fair round figures, such as a Chinese would have placed in his pagoda. I could willingly have dispensed with their attentions; yet, to avoid this, was scarcely within the circle of possibility. All dinner we endured the silliest questions imaginable;

but, that dispatched, away flew your humble servant to the fields and forests. The fathers made a shift to waddle after, as fast and as complaisantly as they were able; but were soon distanced. Now, I found myself at liberty; and ran up a narrow path overhung by rock, with bushy chesnuts starting from the crevices. This led me into wild glens of beech-trees, mostly decayed, and covered with moss; several were fallen. It was amongst these, the holy hermit Gualbertus had his cell. I rested a moment upon one of their huge branches, listening to the roar of the water-fall which the wood concealed: then, springing up, I clambered over crags and fragments, guided by the sound; and, presently, discovered a full stream, precipitating itself down a cliff of pines, amongst which I remained several minutes, watching the falling floods; till, tired with their endless succession, I plunged into the thickest of the grove. A beech received me, like a second Gualbertus, in its hollow trunk. The dry leaves chased each other down the steeps on the edge of the torrents, with hollow rustlings; whilst the solemn wave of the forests above, exactly answered the idea I had formed of Valombrosa,

> *where the'* Etrurian *shades*
> *High overarch't imbowr* . . .*

The scene was beginning to take effect, and the Genius of Milton to move across his favourite valley, when the fathers arrived, puffing and blowing, by an easier ascent than I knew of. Pardon me, if I cursed their intrusion, and wished them as still as Gualbertus. 'You have missed the way,' cried the youngest; 'The Hermitage, with the fine picture by Andrea del Sarto,† which all the English admire, is on the opposite side of the wood: there! don't you see it, on the point of the cliff?' 'Yes, yes,' said I, a little peevishly; 'I wonder the devil has not pushed it down long ago; it seems to invite his kick.' 'Satan,' answered the old Pagod, very dryly, 'is full of malice; but whoever drinks of a spring which the Lord causeth to flow, near the Hermitage, is freed from his illusions.' 'Are they so?' replied I, with a sanctified accent. 'Then prithee conduct me thither, for I have great need of

---

* Milton, *Paradise Lost*, Book I
† Andrea del Sarto (*c.* 1487–1531), celebrated painter of the Florentine school.

such salutary waters; being troubled with strange fancies and imaginations, such as the evil-one himself ought to be ashamed of inspiring.' The youngest father shook his head, as much as to say, this is nothing more than a heretic's whim: the senior, muddled, I conjecture, set forwards with greater piety, and began some legendary tales, of the kind which my soul loveth; rare stories of caves and dens of the earth, inhabited by antient men familiar with spirits, and not the least discomposed by a party of angels coming to dinner, or playing a game at miracles to pass away the evening. He pointed to a chasm in the cliff, round which we were winding by a spiral path, where Gualbertus used to sleep, and, turning himself towards the west, see a long succession of saints and martyrs sweeping athwart the sky, and tinging the clouds with brighter splendors than the setting sun. Here he slumbered till his last hour; when the bells of the convent beneath (which till that moment would have made dogs howl, had there been any within its precincts) struck out such harmonious jingling, that all the country round was ravished, and began lifting up their eyes with singular devotion; when, behold, cherubim appeared, light dawned, and birds chirped, although it was midnight. Alas! alas! what would I not give to witness such a spectacle, and read my prayer book by the effulgence of opening heaven! However, willing to see something at least, I crept into the consecrated cleft, and extended myself on its rugged surface – A very penitential couch! but commanding glorious prospects of the world below, which lay, this evening, in deep blue shade; the sun looking red and angry through misty vapours which prevented our discovering the Tuscan sea. Finding the rock as damp as might be expected, I soon shifted my quarters, and followed the youngest father up to the Romitorio, a snug little hermitage, with a neat chapel, and altar-piece by Andrea del Sarto, which I should have more minutely examined in any other place, but where the wild scenery of hanging woods and meadows, steep hills and nodding precipices, possessed my whole attention. I just staid to taste the holy fountain; and then, escaping from my conductors, ran eagerly down the path, leaping over the springs that crossed it, and entered a lawn of the smoothest turf, grazed by sheep, and swelling into gentle acclivities skirted by groves of fir, whose solemn verdure formed a contrast with its tender green. Beyond this pleasant opening rises a second, hemmed in with copses; and, still higher, a third; from whence a forest of young pines spires up into a lofty theatre, terminated by peaks, universally concealed under a thick mantle of beech, tinged with ruddy brown. Pausing in the midst of the lawns, and looking upward to the sweeps of wood which surrounded me, I addressed my orisons to the Genius of the place, and prayed that I might once more return into its bosom, and be permitted to bring you along with me; for, surely, such meads, such groves, were formed for our enjoyment! This little rite performed, I walked on quite to the extremity of the pastures, traversed a thicket, and found myself on the edge of precipices, beneath whose base the whole Val d'Arno lies expanded. I listened to distant murmurings in the plain, saw smokes rising from the cottages, and viewed a vast tract of barren country, which evening rendered still more desolate, bounded by the high mountain of Radicofani. Then, turning round, I beheld the whole extent of rock and forest, the groves of beech, and wilds above the convent, glowing with firey red; for the sun, making a last effort to pierce the vapours, produced this effect; which was the more striking, as the sky was dark, and the rest of the prospect of a melancholy blue. Returning slowly homeward, I marked the warm glow deserting the eminences, and heard the bell toll sullenly to vespers. The young boys of the seminary were moving in a body to their dark inclosure, all dressed in black. Many of them looked pale and wan. I wished to ask them whether the solitude of Valombrosa suited their age and vivacity; but a tall spectre of a priest drove them along, like a herd, and presently, the gates opening, I saw them no more. A sadness, I could scarcely account for, came over me: I shivered at the bare idea of being cooped up in such a place, and seeing no other living objects than scarecrow priests and friars; to hear every day the same dull service, and droning organ; view the same cloisters; be led the same walks; watched, cribbed, confined, and filled with superstitious terrors. The night was growing chill, the winds boisterous, and, in the intervals of the gusts, I had the addition of a lamentable screech-owl to raise my spirits. Upon the whole, I was not at all concerned to meet the fathers, who came out to show me to my room, and entertain me with various gossipings, both sacred and profane, till supper appeared.

Next morning, the Padre Decano gave us chocolate in his apartments; and, afterwards, led us round the convent, insisting most unmercifully upon our viewing every cell, and every dormitory. However, I was determined to make a full stop at the organ, which is perhaps the most harmonious I ever played upon; but placed in a dark, dingy recess, feebly lighted by lamps, not calculated to inspire triumphant voluntaries. The music partook of the sadness of the scene. The monks, who had all crowded round me, when I first began, in expectation of brisk jigs and lively overtures, soon took themselves away, upon hearing a strain ten times more sorrowful, than that, to which they were accustomed. I did not lament their departure; but played dismally on, till our horses came round to the gate. We mounted; spurred back, through the grove of pines which protect Valombrosa from instrusion; descended the steeps, and, gaining the plains, galloped in three hours to Florence.

Sienna, Oct. 26th
At last, fears were overcome, the epidemical fever at Rome allowed to be no longer dangerous, and myself permitted to quit Florence. The weather was neither gay nor dismal; the country neither fine nor ugly; and your friend full as indifferent as the scenes he looked at. Towards afternoon, a thunder-storm gave character to the landscape, and we entered a narrow vale inclosed by rocks, with streams running at their base. Poplars with faded yellow leaves, sprung from the margin of the rivulets, which seemed to lose themselves in the ruins of a castle, built in the gothic times. Our road led through its court, and passed the antient keep, still darkened by its turrets: a few mud cottages are scattered about the opening, where formerly the chieftain exercised his vassals, and trained them to war. The dungeon, once filled with miserable victims, serves only at present to confine a few goats, which were milking before its entrance. As we were driven along under a tottering gateway, and then through a plain, and up a hill, the breeze whispering amongst the fern which covers it, I felt the sombre autumnal cast of the evening bring back the happy hours I passed last

year, at this very time, calm and sequestered. Full of these recollections, my eyes closed of their own accord, and were not opened for many hours; in short, till we entered Sienna.*

October 27th

Here my duty of course was to see the cathedral, and I got up much earlier than I wished, in order to perform it. I wonder our holy ancestors did not chuse a mountain at once, scrape it into shrines, and chissel it into scripture stories. It would have cost them almost as little trouble as the building in question, which may certainly be esteemed a master-piece of ridiculous taste, and elaborate absurdity. The front, encrusted with alabaster, is worked into a million of fretted arches and puzzling ornaments. There are statues without number, and relievos without end. The church within, is all of black and white marble alternately; the roof blue and gold, with a profusion of silken banners hanging from it; and a cornice running above the principal arcade, composed entirely of bustos, representing the whole series of sovereign pontiffs, from the first bishop of Rome to Adrian the Fourth. Pope Joan figured amongst them between Leo the Fourth and Benedict the Third, till the year 1600, when she was turned out, at the instance of Clement the Eighth, to make room for Zacharias the First . . . Not staying long in the Duomo, we left Sienna in good time; and, after being shaken and tumbled in the worst roads that ever pretended to be made use of, found ourselves beneath the mountains round Radicofani, about seven o'clock, on a cold dismal evening. Up we toiled a steep, craggy ascent, and reached, at length, the inn upon its summit. My heart sank, when I entered a vast range of apartments with high black roofs, once intended for a hunting palace of the Grand Dukes, but now desolate and forlorn. The wind having risen, every door began to shake, and every board substituted for a window, to clatter; as if the severe Power who dwells on the topmost peak of Radicofani, according to its village mythologists, was about to visit his abode. My only spell, to keep him at a distance, was

---

* His unpublished pocket-book reads: 'Think where I was this time year happy and sequestered with my love Wm.' (Pocket-book, 26–31 October 1780, Hamilton Papers.)

kindling an enormous fire; whose charitable gleams cheared my spirits, and gave them a quicker flow. Yet, for some minutes, I never ceased looking, now to the right, now to the left, up at the dark beams, and down the long passages, where the pavement broken up in several places, and earth newly strewn about, seemed to indicate that something horrid was concealed below. A grim fraternity of cats kept whisking backwards and forwards in these dreary avenues, which I am apt to imagine is the very identical scene of the sabbath of witches, at certain periods.

Not venturing to explore them, I fastened my door, pitched my bed opposite the hearth, which glowed with embers, and crept under the coverlids, hardly venturing to go to sleep, lest I should be aroused from it by the sudden glare of torches, and be more initiated than I wished, into the mysteries of the place. Scarce was I settled, before two or three of the brotherhood just mentioned, stalked in at a little opening under the door. I insisted upon their moving off faster than they had entered, suspecting they would soon turn wizards; and was surprized, when midnight came, to hear nothing more than their mewings, doleful enough, and echoed by the hollow walls and arches.

Radicofani, Oct. 28th

I began to despair of magical adventures, since none happened at Radicofani; which nature seems wholly to have abandoned. Not a tree, nor an acre of soil, has she bestowed upon its inhabitants, who would have more excuse for practicing the gloomy art, than the rest of mankind. I was very glad to leave their black hills and stony wilderness behind, and, entering the Papal terrotory, to see some shrubs and corn-fields at a distance, near Aquapadente, which is situated on a ledge of cliffs, mantled with chesnut-copses and tufted ilex. The country grew varied and picturesque. St Lorenzo, the next post, built upon a hill, overlooks the lake of Bolsena, whose woody shores conceal many ruined buildings. We passed some of them in a retired vale, with arches from rock to rock, and grottos beneath, half lost in thickets; from which rise craggy pinnacles, crowned by mouldering towers; just such scenery as Polemburg and Peter de

Laer* introduce in their paintings. Beyond these truly Italian prospects, which a mellow evening tint rendered still more interesting, a
forest of oaks presents itself, upon the brows of hills, which extends
almost the whole way to Mont Fiascone. It was late when we ascended
it. The whole country seems full of inhabited caverns, that began, as
night drew on, to shine with fires. We saw many dark shapes glancing
before them; and perhaps a subterraneous people, like the Cimmerians,† lurk in their recesses. The crackling of flames, and confused
hum of voices, struck our ears, as we passed along. I wished to have
mixed in these nocturnal assemblies; but prudently repressed my
curiosity, lest I might have intruded upon some mysterious rites, and
have suffered the punishment due to sacrilege. As we drew near
Viterbo, the lights in the fields grew less and less frequent; and, when
we entered the town, all was total darkness. Tomorrow I hope to pay
my vows before the high altar of St Peter, and tread the Vatican. My
heart beats quick with the idea of approaching Rome. Why are you
not here to usher me into that imperial city; to watch my first glance
of the Coliseo; and lead me up the stairs of the Capitol? I shall rise
before the sun, that I may see him set from Monte Cavallo.

Rome, Oct. 29th
We set out in the dark. Morning dawned over the Lago di Vico: its
waters, of a deep ultramarine blue, and its surrounding forests catching the rays of the rising sun. It was in vain I looked for the cupola of
St Peter's, upon descending the mountains beyond Viterbo. Nothing
but a sea of vapours was visible. At length, they rolled away; and the
spacious plains began to shew themselves, in which the most warlike of
nations reared their seat of empire. On the left, afar off, rises the rugged
chain of Appenines, and on the other side, a shining expanse of ocean
terminates the view. It was upon this vast surface so many illustrious
actions were performed, and I know not where a mighty people could
have chosen a grander theatre. Here was space for the march of

* Pieter van Laar, known as Il Bambaccio (*c.* 1592–1642), Dutch genre painter who
lived and worked in Rome.
† According to Homer, they were a people who lived near the underworld, on whom
the sun never shone.

armies, and verge enough for encampments. Levels for martial games, and room for that variety of roads and causeways, that led from the Capital to Ostia. How many triumphant legions have trodden these pavements! how many captive kings! What throngs of cars and chariots once glittered on their surface! savage animals dragged from the interior of Africa; and the ambassadors of Indian princes followed by their exotic train, hastening to implore the favour of the senate. During many ages, this eminence commanded, almost every day, such illustrious scenes; but all are vanished; the splendid tumult is passed away; silence and desolation remain. Dreary flats thinly scattered over with ilex, and barren hillocks crowned by solitary towers, were the only objects we perceived for several miles. Now and then, we passed a flock of black, ill-favoured sheep feeding by the way's side, near a ruined sepulchre; just such animals as an antient would have sacrificed to the Manes.* Sometimes we crossed a brook, whose riplings were the only sounds which broke the general stillness, and observed the shepherds' huts on its banks, propped up with broken pedestals and marble friezes. I entered one of them, whose owner was abroad, tending his herds, and began writing upon the sand, and murmuring a melancholy song. Perhaps, the dead listened to me from their narrow cells. The living I can answer for; they were far enough removed. You will not be surprized at the dark tone of my musings in so sad a scene; especially, as the weather lowered; and you are well acquainted how greatly I depend upon skies and sunshine. To-day I had no blue firmament to revive my spirits; no genial gales, no aromatic plants to irritate my nerves, and give at least a momentary animation. Heath and furze were the sole vegetation which covers this endless wilderness. Every slope is strewed with the relics of a happier period; trunks of trees, shattered columns, cedar beams, helmets of bronze, skulls, and coins, are frequently dug up together. I cannot boast of having made any discoveries, nor of sending you any novel intelligence. You knew before how perfectly the environs of Rome were desolate, and how completely the papal government contrives to make its subjects miserable. But, who knows that they were not just as wretched, in those boasted times we are so fond of

* The spirits of the dead, the underworld gods.

celebrating? . . . I could have spent the whole day by the rivulet, lost in dreams and meditations; but recollecting my vow, I ran back to the carriage, and drove on. The road, not having been mended, I believe, since the days of the Cæsars, would not allow our motions to be very precipitate. When you gain the summit of yonder hill, you will discover Rome, said one of the postillions: up we dragged; no city appeared. From the next, cried out a second; and so on, from height to height, did they amuse my expectations. I thought Rome fled before us, such was my impatience; till, at last, we perceived a cluster of hills, with green pastures on their summits, inclosed by thickets, and shaded by flourishing ilex. Here and there, a white house, built in the antient style, with open porticos, that received a faint gleam of the evening sun, just emerged from the clouds and tinting the meads below. Now, domes and towers began to discover themselves in the valley, and St Peter's to rise above the magnificent roofs of the Vatican. Every step we advanced, the scene extended; till, winding suddenly round the hill, all Rome opened to our view. A spring flowed opportunely into a marble cistern close by the way; two cypresses and a pine waved over it. I leaped out, poured water upon my hands, and then, lifting them up to the sylvan Genii of the place, implored their protection. I wished to run wild in the fresh fields and copses above the Vatican, there to have remained, till fauns might peep out of their concealments, and satyrs begin to touch their flutes in the twilight; for the place looks still so wonderous classical, that I can never persuade myself, either Constantine, Attila, or the Popes themselves, have chased them all away. I think I should have found some out, who would have fed me with milk and chesnuts, have sung me a Latian ditty, and mourned the woeful changes which have taken place, since their sacred groves were felled, and Faunus ceased to be oracular. Who can tell but they would have given me some mystic skin to sleep on, that I might have looked into futurity? Shall I ever forget the sensations I experienced, upon slowly descending the hills, and crossing the bridge over the Tyber, when I entered an avenue between terraces and ornamented gates of villas, which leads to the Porto del Popolo? and beheld the square, the domes, the obelisk; the long perspective of streets and palaces opening beyond, all glowing with the vivid red of sun-set? You can imagine how I enjoyed my beloved tint, my favourite hour, surrounded by such objects. You can fancy me ascending Monte Cavallo, leaning against the pedestal which supports Bucephalus; then, spite of time and distance, hurrying to St Peter's in performance of my vow. I met the Holy Father in all his pomp, returning from vespers. Trumpets flourishing, and a legion of guards drawn out upon Ponte St Angelo. Casting a respectful glance upon the Moles Adriani, I moved on, till the full sweep of St Peter's colonade opened upon me, and fixed me, as if spellbound, under the obelisk; lost in wonder. The edifice appears to have been raised within the year, such is its freshness and preservation. I could hardly take my eyes from off the beautiful symmetry of its front, contrasted with the magnificent, though irregular courts of the Vatican, towering over the colonade; till, the sun sinking behind the dome, I ran up the steps, and entered the grand portal, which was on the very point of being closed. I knew not where I was, or to what scene transported. A sacred twilight concealing the extremities of the structures, I could not distinguish any particular ornament, but enjoyed the effect of the whole. No damp air, or fetid exhalation offended me. The perfume of incense was not yet entirely dissipated. No human being stirred. I heard a door close with the sound of thunder, and thought I distinguished some faint whisperings, but am ignorant from whence they came. Several hundred lamps twinkled round the high altar, quite lost in the immensity of the pile. No other light disturbed my reveries, but the dying glow, still visible through the western windows. Imagine how I felt upon finding myself alone in this vast temple, at so late an hour; and think, whether I had not revelations. It was almost eight o'clock before I issued forth, and, pausing a few minutes under the porticos, listened to the rush of the fountains. Then, traversing half the town, I believe, in my way to the Villa Medici, under which I am lodged, fell into a profound repose, which my zeal and exercise may be allowed, I think, to have merited.

October 30th
It was a clear morning; I mounted up to the roof of the house, and sat under a set of open pavilions, surveying the vast group of stately

buildings below; then repaired, immediately after breakfast, to St Peter's, which even exceeded the heighth of my expectations. I could hardly quit it. I wished his Holiness would allow me to erect a little tabernacle under the dome, I should desire no other prospect during the winter; no other sky, than the vast arches glowing with golden ornaments, so lofty as to lose all glitter, or gaudiness. But I cannot say, I should be perfectly contented, unless I could obtain another pavilion for you. Thus established, we would take our evening walks on the field of marble; for is not the pavement vast enough to excuse the extravagance of the appellation? Sometimes, instead of climbing a mountain, we should ascend the cupola, and look down on our little encampment below. At night I should wish for a constellation of lamps dispersed about in clusters, and so contrived as to diffuse a mild equal light for us to read, or draw by. Music should not be wanting; one day, to breathe in the subterraneous chapels, another, to mount high in the dome. The doors should be closed, and not a mortal admitted. No priests, no cardinals; God forbid! We should have all the space to ourselves, and to such creatures too as resemble us. The windows I should shade with transparent curtains of yellow silk, to admit the glow of perpetual summer. Lanterns, as many as you please, of all forms and sizes; they would remind us of China, and, depending from the roofs of the palace, bring before us that of the Emperor Ki; which was twice as large as St Peter's (if we may credit the grand annals) and lighted alone by tapers; for, his imperial majesty, being tired of the sun, would absolutely have a new firmament of his own creation, and an artificial day. Was it not a rare fantastic idea? For my part, I should like of all things to immure myself, after his example, with those I love; forget the divisions of time, have a moon at command, and a theatrical sun to rise and set, at pleasure . . .* I had received no intelligence from England, this many a tedious day; and, for aught I can tell to the contrary, you may have been dead these three weeks. I think, I shall wander soon in the Catacombs, which I am half inclined to imagine communicate with the lower world; and perhaps I may find some letter there from you,

* More or less what was to happen at his unforgettable Christmas party at Fonthill the following year.

lying upon a broken sarcophagus, dated from the realms of Night, and giving an account of your descent into her bosom. Yet, I pray continually, notwithstanding my curiosity to learn what passes in the dark regions beyond the tomb, that you will condescend to remain a few years longer on our planet; for what would become of me, should I lose sight of you? Stay, therefore, as long as you can, and let us have the delight of dozing a little more of this poor existence away together, and steeping ourselves in pleasant dreams.

October 31st

I absolutely will have no antiquary to go prating from fragment to fragment, and tell me, that were I to stay five years in Rome, I should not see half it contained. The thought alone, of so much to look at, is quite distracting, and makes me resolve to view nothing at all in a scientific way; but straggle and wander about just as the spirit chuses. This evening it led me to the Coliseo, and excited a vehement desire in me to break down and pulverize the whole circle of saints' nests and chapels, which disgrace the arena. You recollect, I dare say, the vile effect of this holy trumpery, and would join with all your heart in kicking them into the Tyber. A few lazy abbots were at their devotion before them; such as would have made a lion's mouth water; fatter I dare say, than any saint in the whole martyrology, and ten times more tantalizing. I looked first, at the dens where wild beasts used to be kept, to divert the magnanimous people of Rome with devastation and murder; then, at the tame cattle before the altars. Heavens! thought I to myself, how times are changed! Could ever Vespasian * have imagined his amphitheatre would have been thus inhabited? I passed on, making these reflections, to a dark arcade, overgrown with ilex. In the openings which time and violence have made, a distant grove of cypresses discover themselves; springing from heaps of mouldering ruins, relieved by a clear transparent sky, strewed with a few red clouds. This was the sort of prospect I desired, and I sat down on a shattered frieze, to enjoy it . . . Next, directing my steps to the arch of Constantine, I surveyed the groups of ruins which surrounded me. The cool breeze of

* Vespasian (9–79), emperor of Rome, was an ambitious builder, and began work on the Colosseum.

the evening played in the beds of canes and oziers, which flourished under the walls of the Coliseo: a cloud of birds were upon the wing to regain their haunts in its crevices; and, except the sound of their flight, all was silent; for happily no carriages were rattling along. I observed the palace and obelisk of Saint John of Lateran, at a distance; but it was too late to take a nearer survey; so, returning leisurely home, I traversed the Campo Vaccino, and leaned a moment against one of the columns which supported the temple of Jupiter Stator. Some women were fetching water from the fountain hard by, whilst another group had kindled a fire under the shrubs and twisted fig-trees, which cover the Palatine hill. Innumerable vaults and arches peep out of the vegetation. It was upon these, in all probability, the splendid palace of the Cæsars was raised. Confused fragments of marble, and walls of lofty terraces, are the sole traces of its antient magnificence. A wretched rabble were roasting their chesnuts, on the very spot, perhaps, where Domitian convened a senate, to harangue upon the delicacies of his entertainment.* The light of the flame cast upon the figures around it, and the mixture of tottering wall with foliage impending above their heads, formed a striking picture, which I staid contemplating from my pillar, till the fire went out, the assembly dispersed, and none remained but a withered hag, raking the embers and muttering to herself. I thought it was also high time to retire, lest the unwholesome mists, which were steaming from the opening before the Coliseo, might make me repent my stay. Whether they had already taken effect, or no, I will not absolutely determine; but, something or other gravely discouraged me. A few centuries ago, I should have taxed the old hag with my head-ache, and have attributed the uncommon oppression I experienced, to her baleful power. Hastening to my hotel, I mounted into the open portico upon its summit, nearly upon a level with the Villa Medici, and sat, several hours, with my arms folded in one another, listening to the distant rumours of the town. It had been a fine moment to have bestrode one of the winds which piped round me, offering, no doubt, some compact from Lucifer.

*

* Domitian (51–96) emperor of Rome. After ruling well for some years he gave way to debauchery and great atrocities.

*His mind was ever on the same subject. 'I think I should have signed with
my blood,' he wrote apropos this Luciferian compact, 'such was my desire
to secure a certain object* [Cornaro], *upon that condition, what risks
would I not have run during this fatal moment.'* [10]

November 1st

Though you find I am not yet snatched away from the earth,
according to my last night's bodings, I was far too restless and
dispirited to deliver my recommendatory letters. St Carlos, a mighty
day of gala at Naples, was an excellent excuse for leaving Rome, and
indulging my roving disposition. After spending my morning at St
Peter's, we set off about four o'clock, and drove by the Coliseo, and a
Capuchin convent, whose monks were all busied in preparing the
skeletons of their order, to figure by torch-light, in the evening . . . it
was night when we passed the Torre di mezza via, and began breathing
a close pestilential vapour. Half suffocated, and recollecting a variety
of terrifying tales about the malaria, we advanced, not without fear,
to Veletri, and hardly ventured to fall asleep, when arrived there.

November 2d

I arose at day-break, and, forgetting fevers and mortalities, ran into a
level meadow without the town, whilst the horses were putting to the
carriage. Why should I calumniate the air? it seemed purer and more
transparent than any I had before inhaled. The mountains were
covered with thin mists, and the morning star sparkled above their
summits. Birds were twittering amongst some sheds and bushes,
which border the sides of the road. A chestnut hung over it, against
which I leaned till the chaise came up . . . You will think me gone
wild, when I tell you, I was, in a manner, drunk with the dews of the
morning, and so enraptured with the prospects which lay before me,
as to address them in verse, and compose charms to dispel the en-
chantments of Circe. All day were we approaching her rock: towards
evening, Terracina appeared before us, in a bold romantic scite;
house above house, and turret looking over turret, on the steeps of a
mountain, inclosed with mouldering walls, and crowned by the ruined
terraces of a delightful palace: one of those, perhaps, which the

luxurious Romans inhabited during the summer, when so free and lofty an exposition (the sea below, with its gales and murmurs) must have been exquisitely agreeable. Groves of oranges, and citrons hang on the declivity, rough with the Indian fig, whose bright red flowers, illumined by the sun, had a magic splendor. A palm-tree growing on the highest crag, adds not a little to its singular appearance. Being the largest I had ever seen, and clustered with fruit, I climbed up the rocks to take a close survey of it; and found a spring trickling near its trunk, bordered by fresh herbage. On this I stretched myself by the very edge of the precipice ... Glancing my eyes athwart the sea, I fixed them on the Circean promontory, which lies right opposite to Terracina, joined to the continent by a very narrow strip of land, and appearing like an island. The roar of the waves lashing the base of the precipices, might still be thought the howl of savage monsters; but where are those woods which shaded the dome of the goddess? Scarce a tree appears. A few thickets, and but a few, are the sole remains of this once impenetrable vegetation; yet, even these, I longed to visit; such was my predilection for the spot ... Descending the cliff, and pursuing our route to Mola, along the shore, by a grand road, formed on the ruins of the Appian, we drove under an enormous perpendicular rock, standing detached, like a watch-tower, and cut into arsenals and magazines. Day closed, just as we got beyond it, and a new moon, gleamed faintly on the waters. We saw fires afar off in the bay, some twinkling on the coast, others upon the waves, and heard the murmur of voices; for the night was still and solemn ...

November 3d

The morning was soft, but hazy. I walked in a grove of oranges, white with blossoms, and at the same time glowing with fruit; some of which I obtained leave to gather. The spot sloped pleasantly toward the sea, and here, I amused myself with my agreeable occupation, till the horses were ready: then, set off on the Appian, between hedges of myrtle and aloes, catching fresh gales from the sea as I flew along, and breathing the perfume of an aromatic vegetation, which covers the fields on the shore. We observed variety of towns, with battle-mented walls and antient turrets, crowning the pinnacles of rocky steeps, surrounded by wilds, and rude uncultivated mountains. The Liris, now Garigliano, winds its peaceful course through wide extensive meadows, scattered over with the remains of aqueducts, and waters the base of the rocks, I have just mentioned . . . As soon as we arrived in sight of Capua, the sky darkened, clouds covered the horizon, and presently poured down such deluges of rain, as floated the whole country. The gloom was general; Vesuvius disappeared, just after we had the pleasure of discovering it. Lightening began to flash with dreadful rapidity, and people to run frightened to their homes. At four o'clock, darkness universally prevailed; except when a livid glare of lightning presented instantaneous glimpses of the bay and mountains. We lighted torches, and forded several torrents, almost at the hazard of our lives. The fields round Naples were filled with herds, lowing most piteously; and yet, not half so much scared as their masters, who ran about, cursing and swearing, like Indians during the eclipse of the moon. I knew Vesuvius had often put their courage to proof, but little thought of an inundation occasioning such commotions. For three hours the storm increased in violence; and, instead of entering Naples on a calm evening, and viewing its delightful shores by moon-light; instead of finding the squares and terraces thronged with people, and animated by music, we advanced with fear and terror, through dark streets, totally deserted, every creature being shut up in their houses; and we heard nothing but driving rain, rushing torrents, and the fall of fragments, beaten down by their violence. Our inn, like every other habitation, was in great disorder, and we waited a long while before we could settle in our apartments, with any comfort. All night, the waves roared round the rocky foundations of a fortress beneath my windows, and lightning played clear in my eyes. I could not sleep, and was fully as disturbed as the elements.

November 4th

Peace was restored to nature in the morning, but every mouth was full of the dreadful accidents which had happened in the night. The sky was cloudless when I awoke, and such was the transparence of the atmosphere, that I could clearly discern the rocks, and even some white buildings on the island of Caprea, though at the distance of several miles. A large window fronts my bed, and, its casements being thrown open, gives me a vast prospect of the ocean, uninterrupted, except by the Peaks of Caprea, and the Cape of Sorento. I lay, half an hour, gazing on the smooth level waters, and listening to the confused voices of the fishermen, passing and repassing in light skiffs, which came, and disappeared, in an instant. Running to the balcony the moment my eyes were fairly open (for till then I saw objects, I know not how, as one does in dreams) I leaned over its rails, and viewed Vesuvius, rising distinct into the blue æther, with all that world of gardens and casinos, which are scattered about its base; then, looked down into the street, deep below, thronged with people in holiday garments, and carriages, and soldiers in full parade. The woody, variegated shores of Posilipo next drew my attention. It was on those very rocks, under those tall pines, Sannazaro* was wont to sit by moon-light, or at peep of dawn, holding converse with the Nereids. 'Tis there he still sleeps; and I wished to have gone immediately, and strewed coral over his tomb; but I was obliged to check my impatience, and hurry to the palace, in form and gala. A courtly mob had got thither, upon the same errand, daubed over with lace, and most notably be-perriwigged. Nothing but bows and salutations were going forward on the stair-case, one of the largest I ever beheld, and which a multitude of prelates and friars were ascending in all the pomp of awkwardness. I jostled along to the presence-chamber, where his majesty was dining, alone, in a circular inclosure of fine cloaths and smirking faces. The moment he had finished, twenty long necks were poked forth, and it was a most glorious struggle, amongst some of the most decorated, who first should kiss his hand. Doing so was the great business of the day, and everybody pressed forwards to the best of their abilities. His majesty seemed to eye nothing but the end of his nose, which is doubtless a capital object. Though people have imagined him a weak monarch, I beg leave to differ in opinion; since he has the boldness to prolong his childhood, and be happy, in spite of years and conviction. Give him a boar to stab, and a pigeon to shoot at, a battledore, or an angling-rod, and he is better contented than Solomon in all his glory; and will never discover, like that

*Jacopo Sannazaro (c. 1458–1530), Italian poet, attached to the Neapolitan court.

sapient sovereign, that 'all is vanity and vexation of spirit'. His courtiers, in general, have rather a barbaric appearance, and differ little,
in the character of their physiognomies, from the most savage nations.
I should have taken them for Calmucks or Samoieds, had it not been
for their dresses, and European finery. You may suppose I was not
sorry, after my presentation was over, to return to Sir W.'s, and hear
Lady H. play;* whose music breathes the most pastoral Sicilian ideas,
and transports me to green meads on the sea-coast, where I wander
with Theocritus. The evening was passing swiftly away in this delightful excursion of fancy, and I had almost forgotton there was a
grand illumination at the theatre of St Carlo. After traversing a
number of dark streets, we suddenly entered this enormous edifice,
whose six rows of boxes blazed with tapers. I never beheld such lofty
walls of light, nor so pompous a decoration, as covered the stage.
Marchesi † was singing, in the midst of all these splendors, some of
the poorest music imaginable, with the clearest and most triumphant
voice, perhaps, in the universe. It was some time before I could look
to any purpose around me, or discover what animals inhabited this
glittering world; such was its size and glare. At last, I perceived vast
numbers of ugly beings, in gold and silver raiment, peeping out of
their boxes. The court being present, a tolerable silence was main-
tained; but the moment his majesty withdrew (which great event took
place at the beginning of the second act) every tongue broke loose,
and nothing but buz and hubbub filled up the rest of the entertainment. The last ballet, formed upon the old story of *Le Festin de
Pierre*,‡ had wonderful effect, and terminated in the most striking
perspective of the infernal region. Picq danced incomparably, and
Signora Rossi led the Fandango, with a grace and activity that pleased
me beyond idea. Music was never more rapturous than that which
accompanies this dance. It quite enchanted me, and I longed to have

---

* Sir William Hamilton (1730–1803), was English envoy to the Court of Naples and a
kinsman of Beckford, who was his guest at Posillipo. Lady Hamilton, his first wife, was
soon to become the young man's friend and confidante. A note in Beckford's copy of
his Tour makes it clear that Lady Hamilton's playing this evening was an attempt to
distract two of her Italian guests from offending the company with risqué stories.
† Luigi Marchesi (c. 1750–1829), a popular soprano.
‡ a prose comedy by Molière.

sprung upon the stage. The cadence is so strongly marked by the castanets, that it is almost impossible to be out of time; and the rapidity of steps, and varied movements, scarcely allows a moment, to think of being tired. I should imagine the eternal dance; with which certain tribes of American savages fancy they are to be rewarded in a future existence, might be formed somewhat on this model. Indeed, the Fandango arrived in Spain with the conquerors of the other hemisphere; and is far too lively and extatic to be of European original.

November 6th

Till to-day, we have had nothing but rains; the sea covered with mists, and Caprea invisible. Would you believe it? I have not yet been able to mount to St Elmo, and the Capo di Monte, in order to take a general view of the town. This morning, a bright gleam of sunshine roused me from my slumbers, and summoned me to the broad terrace of Chiaja, directly above the waves, and commanding the whole coast of Posilipo. Insensibly I drew towards it (and you know the pace I run when out upon discoveries) soon reached the entrance of the coast, which lay in dark shades, whilst the crags that lower over it were brightly illumined. Shrubs and vines grew luxuriantly in the crevices of the rock; and their fresh yellow colours, variegated with ivy, had a beautiful effect. To the right, a grove of pines sprung from the highest pinnacles; on the left, bay and chesnut conceal the tomb of Virgil, placed on the summit of a cliff, which impends over the opening of the grotto, and is fringed with a florid vegetation . . . I set myself on a loose stone, immediately beneath the first gloomy arch of the grotto, and, looking down the vast and solemn perspective, terminated by a speck of grey uncertain light, venerated a work, which some old chroniclers have imagined as antient as the Trojan war . . . When I had sat for some time, contemplating this dusky avenue, and trying to persuade myself it was hewn by the Cimmerians, I retreated, without proceeding any further, and followed a narrow path, which led me, after some windings and turnings, along the brink of the precipice, across a vineyard, to that retired nook of the rocks, which shelters Virgil's tomb, most venerably mossed over, and more than half concealed by bushes and vegetation. Drops of dew were distilling from the niches of the little chamber which once contained his urn, and heaps of withered leaves had gathered on the pavement. Amongst these I crept, to eat some grapes and biscuit; having duly scattered a few crumbs, as a sort of offering to the invisible guardians of the place. I believe they were sensible of my piety, and, as a reward, kept vagabonds and clowns away. The one who conducted me, remained aloof, at awful distance, whilst I sat commercing with the manes of my beloved Poet, or straggling about the shrubbery which hangs directly above the mouth of the grot. I wonder I did not visit the eternal shades sooner than I expected; for no squirrel ever skipped from bough to bough more venturously. One instant, I climbed up the branches of a chesnut, and sat almost on its extremity, my feet impending over the chasm below; another, I boldly advanced to the edge of the rock, and saw crouds of people and carriages, diminished by distance, issuing from the bosom of the mountain, and disappearing almost as soon as discovered in the windings of the road. Having clambered high above the cavern, I hazarded my neck on the top of one of the pines, and looked contemptuously down on the race of pigmies, that were so busily moving to and fro . . .

Something of this exalted mood carried over into a letter written the following day to Cozens. 'The Sirens have been propitious and granted me – I am bold and vain enough to say – some few of their persuasive accents – Indeed I flatter myself I have gained considerably,' he wrote, then more modestly, 'how could I do otherwise – hearing Lady Hamilton every day whose taste and feeling exceed the warmest ideas – I pass my whole time with her – she perfectly comprehends me and is more in our style than any woman with whom I am acquainted – My dear little Friend,' he went on, alluding to Courtenay, 'writes me the most affc. Letters I could desire –'[16] It may have been about now that Beckford confided in Lady Hamilton about his affair with Cornaro. Unlike Madame de Rosenberg and Count Benincasa Lady Hamilton was not indulgent, was in fact exceedingly concerned. Beckford was impressed. He had been half-intending to resume the relationship on his way home through Venice where he had already booked his gondoliers and his opera box in anticipation. Now, in face of Lady Hamilton's earnest

*warnings against giving in to the soft alluring of what she quite
definitely considered 'a criminal passion', he temporarily had
second thoughts. Under her benign and gentle influence he began
to make good resolutions, to feel cleansed and innocent once more,
though at a deeper level her condemnation of his passion for
Cornaro only served to confirm him in the belief that unlike other
people he was fated, marked like Gray's poet, to be melancholy for
ever. For the time being however, he continued to enjoy himself, finding the sky bluer and the sun brighter at Posillipo than anywhere else.*

November 8th

This morning I awoke in the glow of sunshine; the air blew fresh and
fragrant: never did I feel more elastic and enlivened. A brisker flow
of spirits, than I had for many a day experienced, animated me with a
desire of rambling about the shore of Baii, and creeping into caverns
and subterraneous chambers. Off I set along Chiaja, and up strange
paths which impend over the grotto of Posilipo; amongst the thickets,
mentioned a letter or two ago: for in my present lively humour, I
disdained ordinary roads, and would take paths and ways of my own.
A society of kids did not understand what I meant, by intruding upon
their precipices; and, scrambling away, scattered sand and fragments
upon the good people, that were trudging along the pavement below.
I went on from pine to pine, and thicket to thicket, upon the brink of
rapid declivities. My conductor, a shrewd savage Sir William had
recommended me, cheered our route with stories that had passed in
the neighbourhood, and traditions about the grot over which we were
travelling. I wish you had been of the party, and sat down by us on
little smooth spots of sward, where I reclined; scarcely knowing which
way caprice was leading. My mind was full of the tales of the place,
and glowed with a vehement desire of exploring the world beyond the
grot. I longed to ascend the promontory of Misenus, and follow the
same dusky route down which the Sybil [prophetess] conducted
Æneas.* With these dispositions I proceeded; and, soon, the cliffs

* Hero of Troy celebrated by Virgil in the *Æneid*, and the legendary founder of Rome.
Several of the emperors of Rome claimed descent from him.

opened to views of the Baian bay, with the little isles of Niscita and Lazaretto, lifting themselves out of the waters. Procita and Ischia appeared at a distance, invested with that purple bloom so inexpressibly beautiful, and peculiar to this fortunate climate. I hailed the prospect, and blessed the transparent air, that gave me life and vigour to run down the rocks, and hie, as fast as my savage, across the plain to Puzzoli. There we took a bark, and rowed out into the blue ocean, by the remains of a sturdy mole: many such, I imagine, adorned the bay in Roman ages, crowned by vast lengths of slender pillars; pavilions at their extremities, and taper cypresses spiring above their ballustrades: this character of villa, occurs very frequently in the paintings of Herculaneum. We had soon crossed over the bay, and landing on a bushy coast, near some fragments of a temple, which they say was raised to Hercules, advanced into the country by narrow tracks, covered with moss, and strewed with shining pebbles; to the right and left, broad masses of luxuriant foliage, chesnut, bay, and ilex, that shelter the ruins of columbariums and sepulchral chambers, where the dead sleep snug, amidst rampant herbage. The region was still, save when a cock crew from the hamlets; which, as well as the tombs, are almost concealed by thickets. No parties of smart Englishmen, and connoisseurs were about. I had all the land to myself, and mounted its steeps, and penetrated into its recesses, with the importance of a discoverer. What a variety of narrow paths, between banks and shades, did I wildly follow! my savage laughing loud at my odd gestures, and useless activity. He wondered I did not scrape the ground for medals, and pocket little bits of plaster, like other plausible young travellers, that had gone before me. After ascending some time, I followed him into the *piscina mirabilis*, the wondrous reservoir which Nero constructed to supply his fleet, when anchored in the neighbouring bay. 'Tis a grand labyrinth of solid vaults and pillars, as you well know; but you cannot conceive the partial gleams of sunshine which played on the arches; nor the variety of roots and ivies trailing from the cove. A noise of trickling waters prevailed, that had almost lulled me to sleep, as I rested myself on the celandine which carpets the floor; but, curiosity urging me forwards, I gained the upper air, walked amongst woods a few minutes; and then, into grots and dismal excavations (prisons they call them) which began to weary me. After having gone up and down, in this manner, for some time, we at last reached an eminence, that looked over the Mare Morto, and the Elysian fields trembling with poplars. The Dead lake, a faithful emblem of eternal tranquillity, looked deep and solemn. A few peasants were passing along its margin, their shadows moving on the water: all was serene and peaceful. The meridian sun played on the distant sea. I enjoyed the pearly atmosphere, and basked in the pure beams, like an inhabitant of Elysium. Turning from the lake, I espied a rock, at about a league distant, whose summit was clad with verdure; and, finding this to be the promontory of Misenus, I immediately set my face to that quarter. We passed several dirty villages, inhabited by an ill-favoured generation, infamous for depredations and murders. Their gardens, however, discover some marks of industry; the fields are separated by neat hedges of cane, and corn seemed to flourish in the inclosures. I walked on, with slowness and deliberation; musing at every step, and stopping ever and anon, to rest myself by springs and tufted bay-trees; when insensibly we began to leave the cultivated lands behind us, and to lose ourselves in shady wilds, which, to all appearance, no mortal had ever trodden. Here, were no paths; no inclosures; a primeval rudeness characterized the whole scene ... The idea of going almost out of the world, soothed the tone of mind, into which, a variety of affecting recollections had thrown me. I formed conjectures about the promontory to which we were tending; and, when I cast my eyes around the savage landscape, transported myself four thousand years into antiquity, and half persuaded myself, I was one of Æneas's companions. After forcing our way about a mile, through glades of shrubs and briars, we entered a verdant opening, at the base of the cliff which takes its name from Misenus. The poets of the Augustan age,* would have celebrated such a meadow with the warmest raptures: they would have discovered a nymph in every flower, and detected a dryad under every tree. Doubtless, imagination never formed a lovelier prospect. Here were clear streams and grassy hillocks; leafy shrubs, and cypresses spiring out of their bosom ... But, as it is not the lot of human animals to be

* The reign of the emperor Augustus (27 B.C.–A.D. 14) saw the flowering of such great poets as Virgil, Horace and Ovid.

contented, instead of reposing in the vale, I scaled the rock, and was three parts dissolved in attaining its summit; a flat spot, covered with herbage, where I lay contemplating the ocean, and fanned by its breezes. The sun darted upon my head: I wished to avoid its immediate influence; no tree was near; deep below lay the pleasant valley; 'twas a long way to descend. Looking round and round, I spied something like a hut, under a crag, on the edge of a dark fissure. Might I avail myself of its covert? My conductor answered in the affirmative; and added, that it was inhabited by a good old woman, who never refused a cup of milk, or slice of bread to refresh a weary traveller. Thirst and fatigue urged me speedily down an intervening slope of stunted myrtle. Though oppressed with heat, I could not help deviating a few steps from the direct way, to notice the uncouth rocks which rose frowning on every quarter. Above the hut, their appearance was truly formidable: dark ivy crept among the crevices, and dwarf aloes with sharp spines, such as Lucifer himself might be supposed to have sown. Indeed, I knew not whether I was not approaching some gate that leads to his abode, as I drew near a gulph (the fissure lately mentioned) and heard the hollow gusts which were imprisoned below. The savage, my guide, shuddered as he passed by, to apprize the old woman of my coming. I felt strangely, and stared around me; and but half liked my situation. To say truth, I wished myself away, and heartily regretted the green vale. In the midst of my doubts, forth tottered the old woman. You are welcome, said she, in a feeble voice, but a better dialect, than I had heard in the neighbourhood. Her look was more humane, and she seemed of a superior race to the inhabitants of the surrounding valleys. My savage treated her with peculiar deference. She had just given him some bread, with which he retired to a respectful distance, bowing to the earth. I caught the mode, and was very obsequious, thinking myself on the point of experiencing a witch's influence, and gaining, perhaps, some insight into the volume of futurity. She smiled at my agitation, and kept beckoning me into the cottage. Now, thought I to myself, I am upon the verge of an adventure. O Quixote! O Sylvio di Rosalva!* how would ye have strutted in such a situation! What fair Infantas

* Sylvio de Rosalva, the eponymous hero of a novel by C. M. Wieland (1733-1813), a quixotic character, who is gradually converted to a doctrine of common sense.

would ye not have expected to behold, condemned to spinning-wheels and solitude? I, alas, saw nothing but clay walls, a straw bed, some glazed earthen bowls, and a wooden crucifix. My shoes were loaded with sand: this, my old hostess perceived; and, immediately kindling a fire in the inner part of the hovel, brought out some warm water to refresh my feet, and set some milk and chesnuts before me. This patriarchal politeness was by no means indifferent, after my tiresome ramble. I sat down opposite the door which fronted the unfathomable gulph; beyond, appeared the sea, of a deep cerulean, foaming with waves. The sky also, was darkening apace with storms . . . Traversing a wild thicket, we soon regained the shore; where I rambled a few minutes, whilst the peasant went for the boat-men. The last streaks of light were quivering on the waters, when I stepped into the bark; and, wrapping myself up in an awning, slept, till we reached Puzzoli; some of whose inhabitants came forth with torches, to light us home. I was vexed to be roused from my visions; and had much rather have sunk into some deep cave of the Cimmerians, than returned to Naples.

Naples, November 9th

We made our excursion to Pompeii, passing through Portici, and over the last lava of Mount Vesuvius. I experienced a strange mixture of sensations, on surveying at once, the mischiefs of the late eruption, in the ruin of villages, farms and vineyards; and, all around them, the most luxuriant and delightful scenery of nature. It was impossible to resist the impressions of melancholy from viewing the former, or not to admit that gaiety of spirits which was inspired by the sight of the latter. I say nothing of the Museum at Portici, which we saw in our way, on account of the ample descriptions of its contents already given to the public; and, because, it should be described no otherwise, than by an exact catalogue, or by an exhibition of engravings. An hour and half brought us from this celebrated repository to Pompeii. Nothing can be conceived more delightful than the climate and situation of this city. It stands upon a gently-rising hill, which commands the bay of Naples, with the islands of Caprea and Ischia, the rich coasts of Sorento, the tower of Castel a Mare; and, on the other side,

Mount Vesuvius, with the lovely country intervening. It is judged to be about an Italian mile long, and three and an half in circuit. We entered the city at the little gate which lies towards Stabiae. The first object upon entering, is a colonade round a square court, which seems to have formed a place of arms. Behind the colonade, is a series of little rooms, destined for the soldiers barracks. The columns are of stone, plaistered with stucco, and coloured. On several of them we found names, scratched in Greek and Latin; probably, those of the soldiers who had been quartered there. Helmets, and armour for various parts of the body, were discovered, amongst the skeletons of some soldiers, whose hard fate had compelled them to wait on duty, at the perilous moment of the city's approaching destruction. Dolphins and tridents, sculptured in relief on most of these relics of armour, seem to shew they had been fabricated for naval service. Some of the sculptures on the arms, probably, belonging to officers, exhibit a greater variety of ornaments. The taking of Troy, wrought on one of the helmets, is beautifully executed; and much may be said in commendation of the work of several others.

We were next led to the remains of a temple and altar, near these barracks. From thence, to some rooms floored (as indeed were almost all that have been cleared from the rubbish) with tesselated, mosaic pavements; of various patterns, and most of them of very elegant execution. Many of these have been taken up, and now form the floors of the rooms in the Museum at Portici; whose best ornaments of every kind, are furnished from the discoveries at Pompeii. From the rooms just mentioned, we descended into a subterraneous chamber, communicating with a bathing apartment. It appears to have served as a kind of office to the latter. It was, probably, here, that the cloaths, used in bathing, were washed. A fire-place, a capacious caldron of bronze, and earthen vessels proper for that purpose, found here, have given rise to the conjecture. Contiguous to this room, is a small circular one with a fire-place; which was the stove to the bath. I should not forget to tell you, that the skeleton of the poor laundress (for so the antiquaries will have it) who was very diligently washing the bathing cloaths, at the time of the eruption, was found lying in an attitude of the most resigned death, not far from the washing caldron, in the office just mentioned ... We now pursued our way through, what is with some probability thought to have been, the principal street. Its narrowness, however, surprised me. It is scarcely eleven feet wide, clear of the foot-ways raised on each side of it. The pavement is formed of a large sort of flattish-surfaced pebbles; not laid down with the greatest evenness, or regularity. The side-ways may be about a yard wide, each paved, irregularly enough, with small stones. There are guard-stones, at equal intervals, to defend the foot-passengers from carriages and horses. I cannot say I found anything either elegant or pleasant in the effect of this open street. But, as the houses in general present little more than a dead wall toward it, I do not imagine any views, beyond mere use and convenience, were consulted in the plan. It led us, however, through the principal gate, or entrance, to a sort of Villa Rustica, without the limits of the city; which amply recompensed our curiosity. The arcade, surrounding a square garden, or court-yard, offers itself first to the observer's notice. Into this, open a number of coved rooms, adorned with paintings of figures, and arabesque. These rooms, though small, have a rich and elegant appearance, their ornaments being very well executed, and retaining still their original freshness. On the top of the arcade runs a walk, or open terrace, leading to the larger apartments of the higher story. One of the rooms below, had a capacious bow-window, where several panes of glass, somewhat shattered, were found; but in sufficient preservation to shew, that the antients were not without knowledge of this species of manufacture. As Horace, and most of the old Latin Poets, dwell much on the praises of antient conviviality, and appear to have valued themselves considerably on their connoisseurship in wine, it was with great pleasure I descended into the spacious cellars, sunk and vaulted beneath the arcade above-mentioned. Several earthen amphorae were standing in rows against the walls; but the Massic and Falernian,* with which they were once stored, had probably long been totally absorbed by the earth and ashes, which were now the sole contents of these venerable jars. The antients are thought to have used oil instead of corks; and that the stoppers were of some matter that could make but little resistance,

* Types of wines. The latter was made from the grapes of Falernus, in Campania.

seems confirmed by the entrance of that, which now supplied the place of wine. The skeletons of several of the family, who had possessed this villa, were discovered in the cellar; together with brass and silver coins, and many such ornaments of dress as were of more durable materials. On re-ascending, we went to the hot and cold baths; thence, to the back of the villa, separated by a passage from the more elegant parts of the house: we were shewn some rooms which had been occupied by the farmer, and from whence several implements of agriculture had been carried, to enrich the collection at Portici. On the whole, the plan and construction of this villa are extremely curious, and its situation very happily chosen. I could not, however, help feeling some regret, in not having had the good fortune to be present at the first discovery. It must have been highly interesting to see all its antient relics (the greater part of which are now removed) each in its proper place; or, at least, in the place they had possessed for so long a course of years. His Sicilian majesty has ordered a correct draught of this villa to be taken, which, it is hoped, will one day be published, with a complete account of all the discoveries at Pompeii . . .

The Tour was sadly drawing to an end, Naples being its southernmost extent. Beckford now forced himself to take a glance at the immediate future, and did not like what he saw. Impending, like the sword of Damocles, was his coming-of-age, and all its consequent responsibilities. Over these the Begum loomed. 'I am now approaching the age when the World in general expect me to lay aside my dreams, abandon my soft illusion and start into public life,' he wrote to Cozens a week after the excursion to Pompeii. 'How greatly are they deceived,' he went on in a burst of petulance, 'how fiercely am I resolved to be a Child for ever.' [17]

For these last few days he had Lady Hamilton to himself: 'I still remain here quiet and happy with Lady Hamilton who is perfectly in our way – we see nobody – Sir Wm. hunts all day long with the King upon the Mountains whilst we indulge our imaginations at home and play strange dreams upon the pianoforte and talk in a melancholy visionary style, which would recall your ancient ideas and fill you with pleasing sadness.' [18]

No doubt Beckford exasperatingly did play strange dreams upon the pianoforte. Lady Hamilton certainly took the opportunity to lecture. Beckford's way home lay through Venice, city of outrageous temptation, and, kind friend as she was, Lady Hamilton was determined to stiffen his flagging resistance. 'I have been just taking a solitary airing during which you have entirely occupied my thoughts,' she wrote a few days after her young guest had left. 'Your singular situation and state of mind makes me feel the anxieties of a Mother and a friend and when I represent to myself the risks you run in various *ways I tremble from head to foot. For Heaven's sake, My Dear Beckford, remember the harsh truths I have often told you; but at the same time remember the affection that dictated them; it was the most painful effort of friendship to say what I have done, and yet I would again repeat it for* your good tho' I felt and still feel *myself the Wounds I gave you and, at this instant that I have your interesting, despairing figure before my eyes as if present. I call myself cruel and cannot refrain from tears, but let them flow. You know how much I have your interest at heart; your honor, reputation and peace of Mind are dear to me, and with a soul like* yours *I am sure you could not enjoy the latter without the former. What would I give to hear the delusion* had ceased and that your mind was as calm as your unfortunate Sensibility would allow —but enough of this; it is in vain to reason with you at this distance ...'* [19] *Beckford, meanwhile had reached Rome. 'My journey was like a dream,' he wrote his hostess. 'Objects passed swiftly and unnoticed before my eyes. Just now the sun set, and the cliffs of Cajeta were glowing with ruddy light. Next instant Monte Circello presented itself and the moon gleamed upon the tranquil waters. A minute after all was darkness and gloom. Sometimes I heard the roar of distant waves, and sometimes undetermined sounds which seemed to issue from the mountains.'* [20]

Rome, December 9th

My last letter was dispatched in such a hurry, that I had not time to conclude it. This will be nearly as imperfect; but yet I cannot forbear writing, having the vanity to believe you are pleased with hearing

* His infatuation for Cornaro.

only, that I am well ... Though enraptured with St Peter's and the
Vatican; with the gardens and groves of pine, that surround this
interesting city; still I cannot help sighing after my native hills and
copses: which look (I know not how it happens) more like the haunts
of Pan, than any I have seen in Italy. I eagerly anticipate the placid
hours we shall pass, perhaps, next summer, on the wild range which
belongs to our sylvan deities. In their deep fastnesses, I will hide
myself from the world, and never allow its glare to bicker through my
foliage. You will follow me, I trust, into retirement, and equally
forget the turmoils of mankind. What have we children of the good
old Sylvanus to do, with the miseries, or triumphs of the savages that
prowl about London? Let us forget there exists such a city; and,
when reposing amongst ivy and blossoms of broom, imagine ourselves
in the antient dominion of Saturn, and dream that we see him pass
along, with his rustic attendants.

*Beckford set out for Venice two days later. It was not the city he had
left. It was now chill and mistbound, and although he insisted on exploring the islands of the lagoon with a determination that exhausted
even the boatmen, his spirits drooped. 'I idle away my mornings in my
gondola wrapped up in furs reading and making calls,' he wrote to a
friend. 'My body is frozen, but my ardent imagination wanders in the
Indies and frolics in the rays of its own sun. The night is spent in
cafés, and at the opera, where Bertoni's voluptuous music, supported
by the artistry of the world's finest singer,* makes me more than ever
effeminate.'* [21]*

*He appears, however, to have been sufficiently armoured by Lady
Hamilton to have resisted the charms of Cornaro. 'Take courage,' she
had written on the 9th of January. 'You have taken the first steps, continue
to resist, and every day you will find the struggle less — the important
struggle — what is it for? no less than* honour, reputation, *and all that
an honest and noble soul holds dear, while infamy,* eternal infamy *(my
Soul freezes when I write the word) attends the giving way to the soft
alluring of a criminal passion.'* [22] *When he reached Augsburg on the 20th
of January he wrote at once to his good angel: 'At length, my dear Lady*

* Pacchierotti.

Hamilton, I am awake and see clearly around me. The gulf into which I was upon the point of being precipitated has disappeared and I am once more calm and happy. It is chiefly to you that I owe this enviable state. Your influence prevailed, your words never ceased to sound in my ears till the good work they had in view was accomplished. To express the transport I feel at my deliverance would be impossible.'[23] On the same day he wrote his last entry of the Tour.

Augsburg, January 20th

For these ten days past, I have been traversing Lapland; winds whistling in my ears, and cones showering down upon my head, from the wilds of pine, through which our route conducted us. Often were we obliged to travel by moonlight; and I leave you to imagine the awful aspect of the Tirol mountains, buried in snow. I scarcely ventured to utter an exclamation of surprize, though prompted by some of the most striking scenes in nature; lest I should interrupt the sacred silence that prevails, during winter, in these boundless solitudes. The streams are frozen, and mankind petrified, for aught I know to the contrary; since whole days have we journeyed on, without perceiving the slightest hint of their existence. I never before felt the pleasure of discovering a smoke rising from a cottage, or of hearing a heifer lowing in its stall; and could not have supposed there would be so much satisfaction in perceiving two or three fur-caps, with faces under them, peeping out of their concealments. I wish you had been with me, exploring this savage region. Wrapped up in our bear-skins, we should have followed its secret avenues, and penetrated, perhaps, into some inchanted cave lined with sables, where, like the heroes of northern romances, we should have been waited upon by dwarfs, and sung drowsily to repose. I think it no bad scheme to sleep away five or six years to come; since, every hour, affairs are growing more and more turbulent. Well, let them! provided we may but enjoy, in security, the shades of our thickets.

· AFTER THE GRAND TOUR ·

1781

Beckford was to enjoy 'the shade of his thickets', a little while longer. By the beginning of February he and Mr Lettice had gained Paris, by March he was in the throes of a heated affair with Georgina Seymour, the high-spirited daughter of Madame du Barry's English lover. At the same time, ever volatile, Beckford was complaining to Cozens of the feeble state of existence to which his passions had brought him. 'Would to God,' he went on, forgetting the warnings and strictures of his good angel in Naples, 'I could snatch up you know who* in my arms and flying to the utmost extremities of the Earth reach that secure retirement of the good old Chinese Monarch supplied by golden fountains eternally flowing with milk.' [1]

The lacteal imagery was not wholly a joke. Like some *dixhuitième* Peter Pan he was viewing with increasing distaste his coming of age at the end of the year, when he would be formally expected to put away childish things and direct his energies to adult matters like supervising his sugar plantations, entering politics, finding a wife. 'I'm still in my cradle!' he moaned apropos to his old friend Madame de Rosenberg. 'Spare the delicacy of my infantile ears, leave me to scamper on verdant banks – all too ready, alas, to crumble, but rainbow-tinted and flower-strewn!' [2]

Soon both Paris and Georgina began to pall, and he found his attention turning nostalgically to William Courtenay, especially when he sat down and played the tunes they had composed together the previous summer. 'You know he was never so happy as when reclined by my side listening to my wild musick, or the strange stories which sprang up in my fancy for his amusement,' he wrote in a lengthy letter to William's young aunt, Charlotte. 'Good God, were he to receive me in coolness and indifference I should desire to close my eyes for ever.' [3]

* Cornaro.

Threatening Lady Hamilton that he would now never be good for anything but writing music, building towers, making gardens and collecting Japan-ware (a self-assessment that was to prove all too accurate) he crossed over to England in April. He no sooner arrived than the invitations began falling 'deep as snow' each morning. Meanwhile Romney began painting his portrait, and, softened perhaps by his encounter with Georgina Seymour, Beckford began falling in love with Louisa, his cousin's wife. Georgina wrote letters threatening to join him. Appalled, Beckford beat a hasty retreat to Fonthill that June, and, with his musician, John Burton, as his only companion, remained safe from intrusion by '*Frenguis*'* as he called undesirables, studying Arabic manuscripts and working on the notes of his Italian tour.

Yet he was also living in a world of perpetual reverie. This found expression in letters that were almost certainly never sent, though they are valuable for revealing his state of mind at the time. Most were concerned with William Courtenay, and are written in a style that brings the nineteenth-century Romantics to mind as he evokes his favourite:

Pale et delicat, les yeux languissant, deviendrà le plus gentil des ombres. Courrones des fleurs de Narcisse vous me venez a cotè de lui. Nous habiterons les mêmes bois, le même gazon nous servirà de lit, on nous trouverà etendû sur les bords de la même fontaine. Le murmure des fleuves eternals calmera s'il est possible les elans de nos ame. Nous seront si penetrè des fautes que l'amour nous a fait commettre, si langoureux et si bleme qu'on n'aura pas le courage de nous faire des reproches [*sic*].' [4]

Into such fantasies the unfortunate Louisa now found herself fatally drawn. In love with Beckford herself, she had to endure the painful confidences concerning his infatuation with young Courtenay, with the result that from this summer onwards she joined the two youths in a dangerously ecstatic trinity.

Like Beckford inclined to melancholy, she began thinking like him. 'There are but few people in the world whom I love,' she wrote. 'The society of others I think an intrusion. How much more pleasing it is

* Feringhee, the oriental word for foreigner.

to sit on the turf under the thick foliage of a spreading tree, thinking on an absent friend, than to converse about la pluye et le beau temps or any other subject equally uninteresting with people with whom you feel the most perfect indifference.'[5] By August she had managed to get rid of her husband who had gone hunting with Mr Drax, and she was at Fonthill, doubtless sympathizing with Beckford over the imminent coming of age, for which elaborate preparations were already going forward.

The subsequent party lasted three days and nights, with more than 10,000 people, 'all neatly dressed', walking the lawns. Tenants were regaled with beer and bands in three tents, those of rarer sensibility being able to listen to the music of woodwinds concealed in thickets, while the *pièce de résistance* of the evening was the *terzetto* sung by Beckford's old friend Pacchierotti, specially imported for the occasion. In both musical and visual effects Beckford had certainly had the major hand. A thousand lamps glimmered in the trees of the Park, while wax torches illuminated the great Fonthill portico and large triumphal arch that had been built opposite. Three enormous bonfires lit up the downs, and from a little classical temple built in an oak grove on a hill-top Beckford surveyed the scene, noting that Fonthill seemed lit by 'a continuous glow of saffron-coloured flame', so that the throng assembled before it looked 'dark and devilish by contrast'. It utterly satisfied his aesthetic soul, 'I rubbed my eyes and thought the whole a dream.'[6]

He was to remain in a state of suspended ecstasy well into the autumn, when he visited Mount Edgecumbe where, standing dreamily on the brink of a cliff with Pacchierotti, he and the singer sang *notturni* into the soft October wind.

By November he was back in London where each Saturday and Sunday he met William Courtenay out from Westminster School to have his portrait painted by Romney. Beckford's mind was now occupied with plans for a grand Christmas party. To this the Begum and her sisters, currently ensconced at Bath with 'fallen mouths and furroughed foreheads', were not to be asked. There were to be only guests of his own choosing.

The subsequent event was without question one of the highlights of Beckford's life. Nearly sixty years later, as an old and embittered man, he still remembered it as 'the realization of romance in its most extravagant intensity'. There is no doubt that his romantic adventures on the Grand Tour had fused a strong eroticism to Beckford's existing sensitivity, so increasing his aesthetic sensibility to that 'passion' which he frequently described as a 'delirium'.

There was everything to indulge such passion at Fonthill that Christmas. Three great *castrati*, Pacchierotti, Tenducci and Venanzio Rauzzini, were engaged to divert Beckford's guests with music, while Jacques de Loutherbourg, among other things a painter of thrilling theatrical scenery, was to produce the visual effects. The guests themselves were to be young, beautiful or interesting. Beckford drove down from London with Cozens and William Courtenay a few days before. 'That night in particular haunts my imagination,' he later wrote Cozens, 'when we arrived from Salisbury and seemed transported to a warm illuminated palace raised by spells in some lonely wilderness. Don't you remember the soft tints that coloured the Thames the preceding evening?'[7] The moment seems to have been one of near-religious ecstasy: never to be forgotten.

Fonthill had been turned into the palace of his most Arabian, most Chinese dreams as he recalled many years later.

Whilst the wretched world without lay bleak and howling, whilst the storm was raging against our massive walls and the snow drifting in clouds, the very air of summer seemed playing around us; the choir of low-toned melodious voices continued to soothe our ear, and, that every sense might in turn receive its blandishment, tables covered with delicious viands and fragrant flowers glided forth by the aid of mechanism at stated intervals from the richly draped and amply curtained recesses of the enchanted precincts.[8]

For three days the members of the house party were thus deliciously immured. It was only in the New Year that rumours began circulating as to what had taken place there.

1782

In the meantime, intoxicated by sensuous memories of vapour of wood of aloes ascending in wreaths, of a glowing haze, of strains of music swelling forth, of the whole mystic look of everything, Beckford rushed into composition. 'I composed *Vathek* immediately upon my return to town,' he later wrote, 'thoroughly embued with all that had passed at Fonthill during this voluptuous festival . . .' [9]

About the side effects of the voluptuous festival the Begum and her sisters were growing increasingly uneasy. 'The Begum is raving at a rate, the prince of the abyss himself has no conception of,' wrote Beckford to Louisa on 11 March, 'whilst Aunt Effingham blows up the flames, and declares it shall no longer be *her* fault if they do not envelope Peter [Louisa's husband] and make him blaze. She tells everybody that comes in her way, royal and unroyal that *she*, at least, is completely scandalized and believes *all* the wild tales which were so charitably circulated of our orientalism last December at Fonthill.' [10]

What actually took place over Christmas will always be a matter for speculation, though it was probably not very much. Some biographers have interpreted certain highly exaggerated letters exchanged between Louisa and Beckford as proof that they were indulging in some form of Black Magic. Certainly the occult had always had a fascination for Beckford, and, along with the occult, the lives of the great and wicked. Since adolescence he had pored over histories like those told of the ghastly sadist, Mulai Isamail, or the loathsome Empress Tanki, 'who,' wrote Beckford in his marginal notes 'used to assemble young people of both sexes, whom she made undress and herself excited to the worst infamies.' [11] Much of the ambience of *Vathek* is drawn from such stories, though the characters of *Vathek* are recognizably autobiographical, and include not only Beckford himself, but his mother and father, Louisa and Courtenay.

As he was writing the adventures of the terrible Caliph, Beckford was plunging into the social whirl of London; flirting with the attractive demi-rep, Lady Craven; composing the music for her opera to which every one of *ton* fought to be invited; dancing at Devonshire House 'bespangled like the rest of the world', he wrote Lady Hamilton as he 'whisked about amongst garlands, lustres and simpering faces till six in the Morning'. [12]

Not everyone approved. Some, while admiring his facility with languages yet criticized his voice, which, for some reason or other, they considered to be like 'that of a eunuch'. Others considered him of so mercurial a turn that he would end his days in a madhouse, yet more resented his gift for satire and mimicry, which made all but the most po-faced laugh. Louisa meanwhile, boxed up in the country, was writing anguished letters dwelling on eternal damnation, the tortures of Hell, the horrors of Death, all of which she was prepared, if need be, to undergo for Beckford's sake. He, by now, was becoming tired of Louisa, and barely found time to answer, unless to engage in the ever-interesting subject of William Courtenay whom they now, for the sake of discretion, nicknamed 'Kitty' in their correspondence.

It was during this time that events took a more active turn, for the Begum, backed by the aunts, had at last perfected a strategy to cope with her wayward son. Louisa, whom she had originally and so mistakenly called upon to distract Beckford from more unsuitable friendships, was to be dropped, nuptial overtures made to Lady Margaret Gordon, a shy but wholesome girl whom Beckford had led out for the first movement of the cotillion at his birthday party. Finally Beckford was once more to be sent abroad, both to keep him out of mischief and to allow time for the injurious rumours concerning the Fonthill Christmas party to die down.

Beckford set out on the 16th of May, this time with a rather more imposing equipage than that of two years ago. In three carriages with postilions rode Mr Lettice, Beckford's private musician, Burton, and Alexander Cozens' son Robert, who was to make sketches of the tour. They were to be away nearly seven months, during which time Beckford's mind scarcely for a moment left its beloved theme.

'You will add many months perhaps years to my life by seeing my lovely Sovereign and filling her head with recollections of our happy hours at Fonthill,'[13] he wrote the long-suffering Louisa three days after they had set out and, 'squashing and sploshing through Meadows and Morasses' at last reached Brussels.

By the time he had reached Augsburg in early June, the weather gloomy, and the mountains capped with snow, he was still dreaming of the Christmas party, and the ecstatic moment by the river at Staines a few days before. 'Burton falls into delightful reveries upon his Harpsichord,' he wrote to Cozens 'but often touches certain chords which bring all Fonthill before my eyes and make me run Wild about the Chamber!'[14] To Lady Hamilton he wrote more coolly the same day, assuring her that he intended to emulate the quiet life led by Milk, her old spaniel. Milk was on his mind, for ten days later in a fit of romantic pique he wrote from Padua, 'They say Gagliani is uncovering at Pompeii. O 'tis a little roundabout gluttonising swinish Animal! that were I an Ogre should be cut into Griskins tho' not for my own Table, I had rather be poor *Milk* with Macaroni and ignorance than Gagliani with Science and Sausages . . .'[15]

At the end of the month he reached Rome where 'cannon were bouncing, trumpets flourishing, the Pope gabbling and Cardinals stinking',[16] and at once lapsed into reverie inviting Louisa in a letter (probably never sent), to remember the three days of Christmas when she, he and Courtenay had reclined on silken beds in the glow of transparent curtains, and how the air had been scented with roses. 'Feed her like a phoenix with perfumes,' he wrote referring to Courtenay in sugared Wildean images. 'Bathe her neck with jessamine and make her observe and glory in observing its whiteness and the blue veins that steal across it. Kiss that swelling bud I am so fond of, and ask her if I may do the same when I return.'[17] Surfeited by what he now regarded as the stiff pines and tiresome vineyards of Italy, he mourned the beech groves of Fonthill, where he and Louisa could have been happy if only some 'fat succubus' would waddle off with her tedious husband.

From Rome he worked his way down to Naples where he instantly went down with a fever. From his bed he wrote how his head was swimming, the room whirling round, the sea turning fantastic colours, and strange islands rising from the waves. When he was strong enough he went on to Lady Hamilton at Portici, spending days lying in a straw hut in a grove of myrtles while Cozens sketched, finding Arabian tales springing up in his head 'like mushrooms on the fresh green downs of Fonthill'.[18] But this pleasant interlude did not last long, for poor Lady Hamilton, always delicate, was dying. By the end of August she had slipped away, and Beckford sadly packed his traps and taking ship for Leghorn began his long journey home. From

Leghorn to Turin, to Geneva, where he stayed with his old friends, the Hubers, then on to Paris, which he reached in October, longing to get back to Fonthill. He reached London on the 10th of November to find a batch of depressing letters from Louisa. She was now so seriously ill with consumption that she had been ordered to the South of France to save her life. She railed bitterly at Fate which had ordained that the moment he should reach England she was about to leave it.

She wrote again on Christmas day, this time by the light of a single taper from a dirty inn in Brignoles, with men boozing in the next room. 'Recollect how we spent this day last year, and think what I must suffer when I compare it with this. Joy and exultation then swelled in every vein, and sparkled in our eyes. K(itty) like a young divinity sat beside us at a table gleaming with silver.'[19]

Beckford himself spent the festival 'very clean and quiet at Fonthill', going through his papers.

1783

He was not to be left long in peace. Before the New Year was a fortnight old the Begum was developing her strategy. The first goal was her son's marriage. 'Has she ceased her persecution or does she still feed Lady Margaret with delusive hopes?' inquired Louisa from Nice, quite unable to take such rumours seriously. As it happened the Begum had correctly assessed matters as they now stood. Not only had the rumours concerning the orientalisms at Fonthill not died down, but an attack was being mounted from another quarter. Throughout February Beckford was complaining to Samuel Henley, his Hamilton cousins' tutor, that the Courtenays were now regarding his friendship with William Courtenay unfavourably. This state of affairs was in part due to the death of the boy's indulgent mother, and the subsequent ascendancy of his aunt Charlotte, now married to Lord Loughborough, a bigoted Scottish lawyer – 'There is something about him,' someone had remarked, 'which even treachery cannot trust.'

Lord Loughborough detested everything Beckford stood for, and was even now misrepresenting him to the boy's father. 'We both live in horrors of that malicious fiend L.L.,' wrote Beckford to Henley, depressed at finding his favourite looking 'pale and meagre as a Portuguese just escaped from the dungeons of the Inquisition'.[20] 'Will they pursue us at every period of our lives?' he asked.

The Begum obviously thought so. Continuing to press for marriage with Lady Margaret she kept a weather eye open for anything that might remotely threaten her son's reputation. It must have been owing to this anxious cast of mind that when the book of the Grand Tour was completed and proudly shown to her that March, she took one look at it and flew into a passion. From this distance in time it is difficult to see quite why it upset her so greatly. Precious it may have been, also whimsical, though for the uninitiated all personal details were sufficiently disguised. Yet she saw in it something that frightened her. A subsequent correspondence reveals that she feared it might outrage the Courtenay family, feared too that Beckford's outspoken comments on the Dutch, with whom England was at peculiar pains to remain friendly, might prejudice him with the political circles she so much wished him to grace. Alarmed perhaps by the Begum's alarm Beckford caved in. On the 15th of April he wrote to Henley ordering him to prohibit the distribution of a book that would have certainly achieved a deserved success in most literary circles. Three weeks later, having informed Louisa only a week before, he married Lady Margaret Gordon by special licence. He was twenty-two, his young wife twenty.

They spent the first night of their honeymoon at Tonbridge. Here he wrote to Cozens, describing their oddly depressing room, heavily wainscoted in cedar, lumbered with chairs gleaming with brass, and how he was staring out of windows before which dark boughs of yew and spruce lashed in the gale. Before the weather had broken he'd seen lights twinkling among distant woods, and, watching the rosy light lingering in the west long after the sun had gone down, had been painfully reminded 'of a certain journey to Fonthill'.[21]

The newly married pair now crossed over to the continent. They were to be away ten months, at the end of which the Begum no doubt hoped all danger would be safely past.

Throughout the honeymoon he continued to live within the continuum of his imagination. 'Every now and then the recollections of past times and happy moments for ever gone, rouses me from my torpid state and forces me to run wildly about on the shore,' he wrote to Cozens from Secheron in June. 'During these moments I dream of Wm. and of Fonthill whilst the confused murmur of leaves and water lulls me to sounder rest. Lady M. walks about gathering flowers from the Shrubs which almost dip their boughs in the Lake. Why am I not happy? – Is it not my own fault that I am miserable?'[22]

The Begum now followed up two resounding successes with mopping-up operations. The relationship between Louisa and Beckford must cease altogether. Incriminating letters had usefully come to hand, and with these she threatened Louisa, unless she agreed never to see or write to Beckford again. 'Never were my senses so cruelly bewildered,' wrote poor Louisa from Vichy '. . . if I must relinquish the happiness of seeing and writing to you, flatter me with the hope that I shall preserve your affection.'[23]

But in defiance of the Begum they continued to maintain a correspondence – anguished on Louisa's side. Meanwhile Beckford's everlasting honeymoon continued, leaving him, as he complained to Cozens, like some melancholy ghost, too full of memories of the world it had left to taste the pleasures of the world into which it was entering. Everywhere the image of Courtenay pursued him. At the same time he could not help feeling a growing affection for his young wife who was now pregnant. 'She is become slender and delicate,' he wrote Louisa. 'Her arms have whitened, their smoothness equals that of your own. The colour which glowed so rudely in her cheeks is softened with a bloom, like the innermost leaves of a blush rose, the more she pines the lovelier she looks . . .'[24]

The pining he alluded to was consequent on further meddling on the part of the Begum who, discovering that she had failed to separate Louisa and her son, had resorted to making Lady Margaret jealous in the hopes that this might force the desired rift. 'Poor Lady M.,' wrote Louisa in November. 'How I pity her if she really feels the horrors of jealousy. She is rather in the situation to inspire it. Were she to see me now, all her fears would vanish and her triumph would be complete . . . Do you and Ly M. occupy the same room?' she inquired, torturing herself. 'Gods! what a question! Fool that I am. Why do I dread the answer. What difference will it make in my situation – can it be more wretched? . . .'[25]

By the time Beckford received her letter he had a sorrow of his own, for some time in October Lady Margaret had miscarried with their first child. Their hopes must have been raised again by the end of November however, since the wretched Louisa, now exiled in Nice, was writing 'How I shall love a little Ganimede *de votre façon!* tho' I must ever regret that it was not my fate to give it birth . . .'[26]

Beckford and his wife now slowly began retracing their steps towards home. The honeymoon, it would appear, had effected an important change in his attitude. Louisa was being replaced in the trinity by Lady Margaret. There was now Beckford, Lady Margaret and William Courtenay. Of William, having just received a letter from him, he wrote to Cozens, '. . . how fortunate am I to have inspired the Object of all my tenderness with so warm and so constant an affection. Neither menaces or sufferings have had any affect . . . Lady M.,' he continued, 'has not the least jealousy . . .'[27]

On the same day that he wrote to Cozens he also wrote to Henley, 'I cannot help thinking you will hear with satisfaction I am happy with Lady M.'[28] 'I am quite impatient for you to see how much I love Lady Margaret,' he was to write Cozens from Paris that December, 'and how totally she is free from prejudice and *wifeishism.*'[29] It was in fact something of a personal triumph for the Begum.

1784

They stayed on at Paris until March, Lady Margaret, in Beckford's words 'waxing more and more like *balloons* every day.'[30] This however did not prevent his dashing round the salons without her in the company of Miss Molly Carter (Moll Volatile to her friends) and Lady Clarges, the trio only condescending to remain when there was, as they judged, no 'fustitude' in the assembled company. They frequently behaved worse than boisterously, Beckford himself deliberately upsetting a glass of water into the furious brocaded lap of Madame Necker.

It was during this period that a radical alteration took place in

Beckford's attitude towards William Courtenay. He had certainly mourned the boy's absence during the early days of his honeymoon, but the following spring he was writing to Sir George Yonge, that in his opinion even the most careful tutoring would not prevent Courtenay being 'a trifling inconsistent character'. Some way along the line it seems that Beckford, like Oscar Wilde, had perceived the wastrel in his favourite. In one of the three episodes of *Vathek*, which he was completing at the time, he was to write of the friendship between Prince Alasi (himself) and the Prince Firouz (Courtenay) and how tyrannical Firouz became, how spoiled, how arrogant, yet Alasi, though he saw this, was powerless, for Firouz 'played on me as he listed'.

Beckford landed at Dover on the 18th of March: 'How I long for the sight of his lovely countenance,'[31] he wrote of Courtenay in the last letter he ever wrote to Cozens. By May he had lost all illusion: 'quite lost in flowers and foolery', he reported brusquely to Samuel Henley, whom he hoped to engage as Courtenay's tutor, '*still more* girlish and trifling than you are aware of'.[32] 'William has been long returned from Devonshire and wastes away in the warm sun of idleness,' he wrote the tutor a fortnight later. 'Don't imagine that I have indulged him as much as appearances a year or two ago might have tempted you to believe,' he continued. 'I am in hopes it will not be difficult for you to fix his attention to objects more worthy of it than balloon hats or silvered sashes.'[33] What was required was more of the *birch* he indicated robustly, and less of the *beechen* shade.

They had both, of course, changed: Courtenay had grown into an unattractive adolescent, Beckford had grown up. His wife was expecting an heir, he had been promised a peerage in preference to becoming a member of parliament, *Vathek* was being prepared for the press. He now did what he could to repair the faults of a character that he had done so much to corrupt.

June saw hopes dashed. The heir to Fonthill was stillborn. Courtenay's father, influenced no doubt by Lord Loughborough, had decided against engaging Henley to tutor his son, and had lit on a Mr Taylor to supervise his boy instead. Yet even at this late stage there was no direct break between the Courtenay and Beckford families, for in September Beckford and Lady Margaret went to stay for a month at Powderham.

The Begum instantly saw danger, and tried to dissuade her son from going, convinced, as she quaintly put it, that Courtenay and Lord Loughborough between them were 'out to lower her son's importance'. As far as Beckford was concerned he arrived at Powderham to find Courtenay 'a poor wretch, more to be pitied than any reptile that crawls the earth, and is mangled, bruised and smashed every day'.[34] Nevertheless, it was now that the incident occurred that gave Lord Loughborough the means by which to ruin Beckford's reputation.

Years after, the Begum confided to the painter, Benjamin West, that Courtenay, through some avoidable carelessness, had exposed an incriminating correspondence that was taking place between her son and Lord Loughborough's wife. Beckford had gone into Courtenay's room to thrash the boy, locking the door. Mr Taylor had reported the incident.

One has heard such explanations, and in the light of the Begum's subsequent suggestion that her son should confound all accusations of homosexuality by running up to London and consorting with the Covent Garden prostitutes, it is difficult to believe in the truth of her story. As it was, Beckford and Lady Margaret left Powderham without apparent incident. A fortnight later however, Beckford was accused of commiting sodomy with the son of the house.

The Begum's next suggestion in the face of this was for Beckford to leave the country. This he agreed to do, and on the 29th of October was at Dover waiting for a passage, though without Lady Margaret, who was once more pregnant. By now, however, he had had time to reflect on the possible effects of such an action, and he decided to reverse his decision and return to Fonthill.

The Courtenay party had meanwhile been browbeating Kitty into making revelations about his friendship with Beckford. The Beckford party had dithered. The only member who had held firm was Lady Margaret: 'I flatter myself,' she wrote to an aunt 'that you cannot disapprove of the part I have taken, sure I was not to abandon *a man* who had always *behaved* to me with *the greatest tenderness and affection* . . .'[35] This in spite of her brother speeding down from Scotland to slap Beckford's face.

But if Lord Loughborough had insufficient evidence to bring a case, he could and did go ahead with the assassination of Beckford's character. On the 27th of November the *Morning Herald* carried a paragraph concerning a rumour of 'a *Grammatical mistake* of Mr B. . . . and the Hon. Mr C. . . . in regard to the genders,' and went on to castigate characters who 'regardless of Divine, Natural and Human law sank themselves below the lowest class of brutes in the most preposterous rites.'[36] Of such rites Lord Pembroke, writing from Italy, was eager to have details. '. . . How, when, and by whom, and with whom discovered? Who passive and who active?'[36]

What appears to have been the quasi-official version of the Powderham affair was retailed from London to Beckford's kinsman, Sir William Hamilton. It was highly inaccurate and ran as follows: Courtenay had been put to school with a clergyman near Fonthill, had been visited very early one morning by Beckford, who had gone into his room. 'Mr Moore,' the tutor, had heard 'a creaking and bustle which raised his curiosity, and thro' the keyhole he saw the operation which it seems he did not interrupt, but informed Lord C. and the whole was blown up.'[37]

Beckford now retreated to the shades of his thickets in good earnest, his peerage cancelled, his reputation lost, ironically enough just as he had seemed set on a fair course at last. He remained with Lady Margaret, exiled, unvisited. Like Oscar Wilde a century later he turned in his anguish, and rent his erstwhile favourite. 'Let it suffice for me to assure you,' he wrote Henley, 'that a certain young person I once thought my friend has proved himself the meanest traitor and blackest enemy. You may guess,' he continued, 'who moved the wires and made this miserable puppet dance to its destruction.'[38]

As he was to write several years later, it was now that he began to dream of extending his forests, and of 'sticking them full of hideous iron traps and spring guns that would snap off legs as neatly as Pinchbeck's patent snuffers snuffed candles. In process of time when my hills are completely blackened with fir,' he continued, 'I shall retreat into the center of this gloomy circle, like a spider into the midst of his web . . .'[39] It was a metaphor for what was indeed to happen. He was twenty-four.

· POSTSCRIPT ·

Beckford survived. Psychologically perhaps only just. Yet such were his powers of recuperation that seven years after the debacle Mrs Piozzi could remark with amazement that people seemed to have forgotten everything else about him bar the fact that he was 'an *Authour*. What a world it is!!!' [1] she commented tiredly.

In the seven years he gained two daughters and lost his wife in childbirth. His novel, *Vathek*, was published. Restless as ever, he set out for the West Indies, found the ship crawling with cockroaches, fumigated it, filled it with geraniums, but was so sick in the Bay that he got off at Lisbon and remained there. Here, in spite of unfriendly opposition from the British Minister at the Court, he soon became the talk of the town, and the close friend of the influential Marialva family. Infatuations in the old style followed, the boy Franchi, another boy, known only as the 'malheureux Ki-Ki', Dom Pedro Marialva himself, the Marquesa de Sala. Yet time hung heavy. 'Every day is tinted with the same dull colours,' [2] he wrote, and moved on to Paris. Here rumours of an imminent attack on the Tuileries forced him to decamp hastily to Savoy, though not before adding the clarinets, oboes and drums of the Garde du Roy to his baggage train.

From this time onwards (November 1792) his life assumed an increasingly legendary quality. He appears to have been trapped in Jacobin Paris during which some reported his being present at the execution of the King, while others affirmed that, disguised as a bookseller's assistant, he had served over the counter in Mérigot's shop. Whatever the truth he was back in Lisbon by autumn 1793, Fonthill in winter 1796, making plans to set up as negotiator for a Peace between England and France in the hopes of being rewarded with the peerage he had lost. The project came to nothing, and he turned his attention to Fonthill once more. 'I grow rich and mean to build towers,' [3] he wrote, and, with Wyatt as architect, began work on an entire Abbey complete with courts, cloisters, dining-hall, a chapel dedicated to St Anthony, and a tower that was to be higher than that of Salisbury Cathedral. Here, where sixty fires in filigree baskets filled with perfumed coal were kept constantly burning, he shortly withdrew in accordance with his favourite motto, *Secret et Heureux*, entertaining only those artists and men of letters who interested him, and forbidding entry to the growing number of curiosity seekers.

Meanwhile five hundred workmen working in gangs day and night raised the triumphant three-hundred-foot tower. Alas, not many months later, there was a freak gale and the jerrybuilt structure slid to the ground. 'We shall rise again more gloriously,'[4] promised Beckford, undismayed. The following December the building was completed, and to the strains of 'Rule, Britannia!' and 'God Save the King' Beckford entertained Lord Nelson, his kinsman, Sir William Hamilton and his second wife, the notorious and beautiful Emma. The grand dinner was served in the Great Hall 'in one long line of silver dishes,' it was reported, 'in the substantial costume of the antient abbeys, unmixed with the refinement of modern cookery.'[5]

News of this and other goings on, which included rumours of orgies, dwarves and black magic, filtered to an outer world passionate to catch a glimpse of the eccentric millionaire. In 1809 Byron, (a fervent admirer) while changing horses at Hartford Bridge heard that Beckford, 'the martyr of prejudice', was staying in the inn, though he was unable to catch sight of him. It is from Byron that we learn that by some strange stroke of chance Courtenay, now forty-one, was travelling the same road as Beckford that very night, 'only one stage *behind* him',[6] as the poet maliciously expressed it.

They had not met since 1784, during which time the unattractive characteristics that Beckford had already discerned in his one-time favourite, had come into full bloom. Courtenay's reputation over the years had grown so murky that when he attempted to build a house near Torquay, the townsfolk drummed his workmen out of the parish. By 1811 rumours so outrageous had collected round him that he was forced to flee to France under an assumed name to escape arrest. He never came back.

Beckford meanwhile was beginning to feel the consequences of a prolonged and vast expenditure. In 1820 people were astounded to hear that the Abbey was up for sale. 72,000 copies of the sale catalogue were sold, and coachloads of sightseers travelled into Wiltshire to see for themselves the wonders of the Abbey and its contents, while Beckford himself coolly withdrew to Bath with Tiny, his favourite spaniel.

He was now sixty-three. Bath gossips told strangers that there were no looking-glasses permitted in the house at Lansdowne Crescent, that, disliking women, the Master had had niches constructed along passages and stairways into which maids might cower as he went past. Occasionally he was seen setting out for an excursion, his steward riding ahead, followed by two grooms armed with long whips, after which, surrounded by a cloud of dogs, rode Beckford. Like some eighteenth-century *revenant* he dressed in an old-fashioned green coat, frills, white neckcloth, boots and knee-breeches. Two more grooms brought up the rear.

It was not long before he was building another tower, still to be seen today on the crest of Lansdowne Hill, and round it creating a delectable garden out of an old stone-quarry and waste ground. Here were no parterres nor neatly-clipped walks, according to his acquaintance, Cyrus Redding, but thickets of sweet-smelling roses, turf walks planted with thyme and marjoram, and shady groves of fig trees leading to secret grottoes and ferny pools. Beckford rode up here each morning after a cup of chicken broth, to spend his day pottering among his plants and discussing plans with Vincent, his eighty-year-old gardener, and every day he arranged fresh flowers in an ivory vase lined with crystal that stood in the tower.

His retirement was not always tranquil. Three years after arriving in Bath he determined to visit Rome once more, and for five months he made extensive preparations. New carriages were specially built and stocked with wines and Bristol water. New servants' liveries were ordered, and cooks and couriers specially engaged. The caravan set out in August with Beckford riding at its head. The weather was exceedingly hot, and by the time they reached Marlborough Beckford was suffering from sunburn. His dressing gown it seems, had been mislaid, he flew into an apopleptic fury, the servants were terrified.

The next day they somehow pushed on to London, but by the time they arrived, the Caliph had changed his mind. He would return to Bath, his garden and Tiny.

As the pampered years went by, he became ever more irascible, volatile, malicious, and these unpleasing characteristics flashed forth in innumerable spiteful and petty acts. He had long ago bought and locked away from public sight the library of Gibbon, which the historian had hoped to make available to the world. He now delighted in running up prices at the book auctions he attended, leaving prospective buyers to extricate themselves at the top of the bid, or he would put in an offer for some worthless painting in the hope that some dealer, banking on his reputation for impeccable taste might be trapped into buying something that was valueless. He spent hours, like some evil old troll, poring over what he called his *Liber Veritatis* in which, against the genealogies of the great, he noted every old scandal and bent pedigree he could snuff out, and in the margins of the books he read he pencilled voluminous and acrid comments. Of Gibbon: '. . . the prurient and obscene gossip of your notes – your affected moral purity perking up every now and then from the corrupt mass like artificial roses shaken off in the dark by some Prostitute on a heap of manure . . .'[7]; of Mary Wollstonecraft's *Frankenstein*: 'This is perhaps the foulest Toadstool that has yet sprung up from the reeking dunghill of the present times.'[8] All lady writers (whom he detested) were advised to stick to cross-stitch and yabble-stitch to save people like him from their interminable 'scribbleations'.

So he relieved his bile for the next eighteen years. He continued to collect books and prints, though by now from mere habit rather than interest. He continued too to intrigue for the coronet for which he ever hoped. He read Disraeli's *Contarini Fleming*, and for a brief moment was so charmed, thinking to have at last found a kindred spirit, that he arranged a meeting.

'Beckford very bitter and *malin*,'[9] wrote Disraeli of this encounter which lasted three hours. Beckford on his part soon cooled. He retired to examine his own works, in particular the travel diaries. He began slowly and painstakingly to edit these journeys to Italy, to Spain, to Portugal, censoring a passage here, inserting an anecdote there, and in

1834 published them and grew heady with the champagne of an enthusiastic acclaim. He began reconsidering his letters, reshaping, rewriting, transforming his long sad egotistical life into something approaching a work of art.

Tiny had died. Beckford now built himself a mausoleum in glittering pink granite beside Tiny's grave and round it planted his favourite flowers.

In 1843 at the age of eighty-three, he had a bout of fever and nearly died, but just managed to pull through. The following year he got soaked returning from a long excursion and fever once more set in. It appears that he felt suddenly lonely. 'Quick! Come quick!' he wrote to his one daughter who was not estranged. She came, bringing with her an Anglican parson whom Beckford refused to see. At ten o'clock on the morning of the 2nd of May 1844 he became unconscious. An hour later he died.

'Lead me to another world of dangers,' he had written long, long ago, when he had been a gifted boy of seventeen with all the world before him. 'Let me be plunged anew into the terrors of initiation if they do but lead to the last.'

'Repress', said Moisasour,* 'so daring a curiosity. This last initiation is Death.' [10]

* One of Beckford's own characters.

· SOURCES ·

MANUSCRIPT SOURCES

The Beckford Papers: These are now in the Bodleian Library at Oxford, and are in the process of being re-catalogued. My references follow the system of cataloguing used when the papers were in the possession of the Duke of Hamilton, hence I refer to the *Hamilton Papers*, and in particular to *The Red Copy Book* in that collection, which contains transcripts of Beckford's letters.

BOOKS

Alexander, Boyd, *England's Wealthiest Son: A Study of William Beckford*. London 1962
Chapman, Guy, *Beckford*. London 1937.
Fothergill, Brian, *Beckford of Fonthill*. London 1979.

ABBREVIATIONS

Alexander   *England's Wealthiest Son*, by Boyd Alexander
Chapman   *Beckford*, by Guy Chapman
Fothergill   *Beckford of Fonthill*, by Brian Fothergill
HP   *Hamilton Papers*
RCB   *Red Copy Book*

· NOTES ·

INTRODUCTION

1 Letters of Horace Walpole, ed. Toynbee (Oxford, 1903), Vol. I, p. 36.

2 *ibid.*, p. 41

3 *Dreams, Waking Thoughts and Incidents*, Letter VIII

4 *Italian Landscape in Eighteenth Century England*, Manwaring, Elizabeth Wheeler (London, 1925), p. 28

5 *ibid.*, p. 31

6 *ibid.*, p. 31

7 HP, English Journal 1779

8 HP, Travel Journal for Oct. 1780

9 HP, RCB No. 50, Fonthill, Aug. 31 1781

10 HP, RCB No. 16, From the Summit of the Mountain of Salève, 9 o'clock Sept. 13 1777

11 HP, RCB No. 7, Fonthill, December 4th 1778, being the full of the Moon

12 HP, RCB No. 10, to Alexander Cozens, Friday, 8 o'clock Eve. Dec. 3rd 1779

13 HP, Travel Journal for Oct. 1780

14 HP, English Journal 1779

15 *Dreams, Waking Thoughts and Incidents*, Letter VIII

16 *Dreams, Waking Thoughts and Incidents*, Letter XXVII

BEFORE THE GRAND TOUR

1 Chapman, p. 34

2 *ibid.*, p. 35

3 *ibid.*, p. 39

4 *ibid.*, p. 39

5 Alexander, p. 43

6 *ibid.*, p. 46

7 *ibid.*, p. 67

8 Fothergill, p. 64
9 Chapman, p. 50
10 *ibid.*, p. 44
11 HP, Satyrs range. Fonthill, August 1779
12 Fothergill, p. 55
13 Chapman, p. 55
14 Fothergill, p. 74
15 Alexander, p. 70

THE GRAND TOUR

1 HP, RCB No. 32, Margate, June 20 1780
2 Fothergill, p. 81
3 HP, RCB No. 31, Hague, June 29 1780
4 HP, RCB No. 28, Spá, July 7 1780
5 Chapman, p. 69
6 *ibid.*, p. 69
7 Fothergill, p. 87
8 Alexander, p. 76
9 Heriot, Angus, *The Castrati in Opera* (London, 1956), p. 167
10 *ibid.*, p. 170
11 Fothergill, p. 90
12 Heriot, p. 14
13 *ibid.*, p. 44
14 *ibid.*, p. 54
15 Chapman, p. 72
16 Fothergill, p. 94
17 *ibid.*, p. 96
18 HP, RCB No. 34, Caserta, November 30 1780
19 Fothergill, p. 96
20 Chapman, p. 78
21 Alexander, p. 78
22 Chapman, p. 78
23 Fothergill, p. 87

AFTER THE GRAND TOUR

1 HP, RCB No. 30, either to Louisa or Alexander Cozens, March 10th 1781

2 Fothergill, p. 104

3 Chapman, p. 82

4 Alexander, p. 266

5 Chapman, p. 95

6 Alexander, p. 80

7 Fothergill, p. 112

8 Alexander, p. 81

9 Fothergill, p. 115

10 *ibid*., p. 121

11 Alexander, p. 85

12 HP, RCB No. 36, to Lady Hamilton, London, March 26 1782

13 HP, RCB No. 20, to Louisa, Brussels, May 19th 1782

14 HP, RCB No. 22, to Alexander Cozens, Augsburg, June 2nd 1782

15 HP, RCB No. 39, to Lady Hamilton, Padua, June 13th 1782

16 HP, RCB No. 18, to his cousin, Mr Hamilton, Rome, June 29th 1782

17 HP, RCB No. 59, to Louisa, Rome, June 30th 1782

18 Chapman, p. 140

19 *ibid*., p. 143

20 *ibid*., p. 146

21 HP, RCB No. 52, to Alexander Cozens, Tunbridge, Wed., May 1783

22 Chapman, p. 157

23 *ibid*., p. 157

24 *ibid*., p. 165

25 *ibid*., p. 166

26 *ibid*., p. 167

27 *ibid*., p. 168

28 *ibid*., p. 168

29 *ibid*., p. 170

30 *ibid*., p. 178

31 *ibid*., p. 178

32 *ibid*., p. 179

33 *ibid*., p. 179

34 *ibid*., p. 182

35 Fothergill, p. 172

36 Chapman, p. 185

37 Fothergill, p. 173

38 *ibid*., p. 173

39 *ibid*., p. 177

40 Alexander, p. 122

POSTSCRIPT

1 *Thraliana, The Diary of Mrs. Hester Lynch Thrale*, ed. Katherine C. Balderstone (London, 1951), Vol II. p. 799
2 Chapman, p. 216
3 *ibid.*, p. 234
4 *ibid.*, p. 268
5 *ibid.*, p. 273
6 *ibid.*, p. 275
7 *ibid.*, p. 303
8 *ibid.*, p. 305
9 *ibid.*, p. 317
10 *ibid.*, p. 290

ACKNOWLEDGEMENTS

I should like to thank Mr Tim Rogers of the Bodleian Library for his kind help with the Beckford Papers (particularly as he was fully occupied in cataloguing them at the time), and Judith Flanders of Penguin Books.

· INDEX ·

MORE ABOUT PENGUINS, PELICANS, PEREGRINES AND PUFFINS

For further information about books available from Penguins please write to Dept EP, Penguin Books Ltd, Harmondsworth, Middlesex UB7 ODA.

In the U.S.A.: For a complete list of books available from Penguins in the United States write to Dept DG, Penguin Books, 299 Murray Hill Parkway, East Rutherford, New Jersey 07073.

In Canada: For a complete list of books available from Penguins in Canada write to Penguin Books Canada Limited, 2801 John Street, Markham, Ontario L3R 1B4.

In Australia: For a complete list of books available from Penguins in Australia write to the Marketing Department, Penguin Books Australia Ltd, P.O. Box 257, Ringwood, Victoria 3134.

In New Zealand: For a complete list of books available from Penguins in New Zealand write to the Marketing Department, Penguin Books (N.Z.) Ltd, Private Bag, Takapuna, Auckland 9.

In India: For a complete list of books available from Penguins in India write to Penguin Overseas Ltd, 706 Eros Apartments, 56 Nehru Place, New Delhi 110019.

Elizabeth Mavor in Penguins

THE LADIES OF LLANGOLLEN

Depicting a friendship that lasted over fifty years, Elizabeth Mavor's beautifully detailed biography gives us a fascinating glimpse into the life and times of two remarkable women.

Lady Eleanor Butler was twenty-nine when she first met Sarah Ponsonby, a sensitive, retiring girl of thirteen. Ten years later, in 1778, the two ladies eloped.

Amid scenes of scandal and havoc they settled in an idyllic cottage in Llangollen where their unorthodox relationship blossomed, and their generous, civilized way of living became a legend: Lady Caroline Lamb and Josiah Wedgwood visited them, Wordsworth and Southey wrote poetry under their roof, and other celebrities of the day, such as the Duke of Wellington, became cherished friends.

'They were two people of extraordinary courage ... it's a very moving book and it's also very funny' – Paul Bailey

Elizabeth Mavor in Penguins

A YEAR WITH THE LADIES OF LLANGOLLEN

In 1778, to the fury of their aristocratic families, Eleanor Butler and Sarah Ponsonby eloped and fled to North Wales, to Llangollen.

This charming book is taken from the journal that Eleanor Butler kept of their life together. During their lifetime, its contents aroused much speculation, but no one was permitted to see it and its true nature was protected from prying eyes. In fact, the journal is a delightful record of the ladies' devotion to one another and of the times in which they lived.

Elizabeth Mavor's selection includes extracts from the journals themselves, and from the Ladies' Receipt and Account Books, together with a number of unpublished letters, all giving an extraordinarily vivid picture of village life in the late eighteenth century and of the remarkable friendship of the Ladies of Llangollen.

Published in hardback under the title, *Life with the Ladies of Llangollen*.

PENGUIN TRAVEL BOOKS

☐ *Arabian Sands* **Wilfred Thesiger**   £3.95

'In the tradition of Burton, Doughty, Lawrence, Philby and Thomas, it is, very likely, the book about Arabia to end all books about Arabia' – *Daily Telegraph*

☐ *The Flight of Ikaros* **Kevin Andrews**   £3.50

'He also is in love with the country . . . but he sees the other side of that dazzling medal or moon ... If you want some truth about Greece, here it is' – Louis MacNeice in the *Observer*

☐ *D. H. Lawrence and Italy*   £4.95

In *Twilight in Italy, Sea and Sardinia* and *Etruscan Places,* Lawrence recorded his impressions while living, writing and travelling in 'one of the most beautiful countries in the world'.

☐ *Maiden Voyage* **Denton Welch**   £3.95

Opening during his last term at public school, from which the author absconded, *Maiden Voyage* turns into a brilliantly idiosyncratic account of China in the 1930s.

☐ *The Grand Irish Tour* **Peter Somerville-Large**   £4.95

The account of a year's journey round Ireland. 'Marvellous ... describes to me afresh a landscape I thought I knew' – Edna O'Brien in the *Observer*

☐ *Slow Boats to China* **Gavin Young**   £3.95

On an ancient steamer, a cargo dhow, a Filipino kumpit and twenty more agreeably cranky boats, Gavin Young sailed from Piraeus to Canton in seven crowded and colourful months. 'A pleasure to read' – Paul Theroux

PENGUIN TRAVEL BOOKS

☐ *The Kingdom by the Sea* **Paul Theroux**   **£2.50**

1982, the year of the Falklands War and the Royal Baby, was the ideal time, Theroux found, to travel round the coast of Britain and surprise the British into talking about themselves. 'He describes it all brilliantly and honestly' – Anthony Burgess

☐ *One's Company* **Peter Fleming**   **£3.50**

His journey to China as special correspondent to *The Times* in 1933. 'One reads him for literary delight . . . But, he is also an observer of penetrating intellect' – Vita Sackville West

☐ *The Traveller's Tree* **Patrick Leigh Fermor**   **£3.95**

'A picture of the Indies more penetrating and original than any that has been presented before' – *Observer*

☐ *The Path to Rome* **Hilaire Belloc**   **£3.95**

'The only book I ever wrote for love,' is how Belloc described the wonderful blend of anecdote, humour and reflection that makes up the story of his pilgrimage to Rome.

☐ *The Light Garden of the Angel King* **Peter Levi**   **£2.95**

Afghanistan has been a wild rocky highway for nomads and merchants, Alexander the Great, Buddhist monks, great Moghul conquerors and the armies of the Raj. Here, quite brilliantly, Levi writes about their journeys and his own.

☐ *Among the Russians* **Colin Thubron**   **£3.95**

'The Thubron approach to travelling has an integrity that belongs to another age' – Dervla Murphy in the *Irish Times*. 'A magnificent achievement' – Nikolai Tolstoy

A CHOICE OF PENGUINS

☐ **The Complete Penguin Stereo Record and Cassette Guide**
Greenfield, Layton and March £7.95

A new edition, now including information on compact discs. 'One of the few indispensables on the record collector's bookshelf' – *Gramophone*

☐ **Selected Letters of Malcolm Lowry**
Edited by Harvey Breit and Margerie Bonner Lowry £5.95

'Lowry emerges from these letters not only as an extremely interesting man, but also a lovable one' – Philip Toynbee

☐ **The First Day on the Somme**
Martin Middlebrook £3.95

1 July 1916 was the blackest day of slaughter in the history of the British Army. 'The soldiers receive the best service a historian can provide: their story told in their own words' – *Guardian*

☐ **A Better Class of Person** **John Osborne** £2.50

The playwright's autobiography, 1929–56. 'Splendidly enjoyable' – John Mortimer. 'One of the best, richest and most bitterly truthful autobiographies that I have ever read' – Melvyn Bragg

☐ **The Winning Streak** **Goldsmith and Clutterbuck** £2.95

Marks & Spencer, Saatchi & Saatchi, United Biscuits, GEC . . . The UK's top companies reveal their formulas for success, in an important and stimulating book that no British manager can afford to ignore.

☐ **The First World War** **A. J. P. Taylor** £4.95

'He manages in some 200 illustrated pages to say almost everything that is important . . . A special text . . . a remarkable collection of photographs' – *Observer*

A CHOICE OF PENGUINS

☐ *Man and the Natural World* **Keith Thomas**   **£4.95**

Changing attitudes in England, 1500–1800. 'An encyclopedic study of man's relationship to animals and plants ... a book to read again and again' – Paul Theroux, *Sunday Times* Books of the Year

☐ *Jean Rhys: Letters 1931–66*
  Edited by Francis Wyndham and Diana Melly   **£4.95**

'Eloquent and invaluable ... her life emerges, and with it a portrait of an unexpectedly indomitable figure' – Marina Warner in the *Sunday Times*

☐ *The French Revolution* **Christopher Hibbert**   **£4.95**

'One of the best accounts of the Revolution that I know ... Mr Hibbert is outstanding' – J. H. Plumb in the *Sunday Telegraph*

☐ *Isak Dinesen* **Judith Thurman**   **£4.95**

The acclaimed life of Karen Blixen, 'beautiful bride, disappointed wife, radiant lover, bereft and widowed woman, writer, sibyl, Scheherazade, child of Lucifer, Baroness; always a unique human being ... an assiduously researched and finely narrated biography' – *Books & Bookmen*

☐ *The Amateur Naturalist*
  Gerald Durrell with Lee Durrell   **£4.95**

'Delight ... on every page ... packed with authoritative writing, learning without pomposity ... it represents a real bargain' – *The Times Educational Supplement.* 'What treats are in store for the average British household' – *Daily Express*

☐ *When the Wind Blows* **Raymond Briggs**   **£2.95**

'A visual parable against nuclear war: all the more chilling for being in the form of a strip cartoon' – *Sunday Times.* 'The most eloquent anti-Bomb statement you are likely to read' – *Daily Mail*

CLASSICS IN TRANSLATION
IN PENGUINS

☐ *Remembrance of Things Past* **Marcel Proust**

☐ Volume One: *Swann's Way, Within a Budding Grove*   £7.95
☐ Volume Two: *The Guermantes Way, Cities of the Plain*   £7.95
☐ Volume Three: *The Captive, The Fugitive, Time Regained*   £7.95

Terence Kilmartin's acclaimed revised version of C. K. Scott Moncrieff's original translation, published in paperback for the first time.

☐ *The Canterbury Tales* **Geoffrey Chaucer**   £2.95

'Every age is a Canterbury Pilgrimage . . . nor can a child be born who is not one of these characters of Chaucer' – William Blake

☐ *Gargantua & Pantagruel* **Rabelais**   £3.95

The fantastic adventures of two giants through which Rabelais (1495–1553) caricatured his life and times in a masterpiece of exuberance and glorious exaggeration.

☐ *The Brothers Karamazov* **Fyodor Dostoevsky**   £4.95

A detective story on many levels, profoundly involving the question of the existence of God, Dostoevsky's great drama of parricide and fraternal jealousy triumphantly fulfilled his aim: 'to find the man in man . . . [to] depict all the depths of the human soul.'

☐ *Fables of Aesop*   £1.95

This translation recovers all the old magic of fables in which, too often, the fox steps forward as the cynical hero and a lamb is an ass to lie down with a lion.

☐ *The Three Theban Plays* **Sophocles**   £2.95

A new translation, by Robert Fagles, of *Antigone, Oedipus the King* and *Oedipus at Colonus*, plays all based on the legend of the royal house of Thebes.

CLASSICS IN TRANSLATION
IN PENGUINS

☐ *The Treasure of the City of Ladies*
Christine de Pisan   £2.95

This practical survival handbook for women (whether royal courtiers
or prostitutes) paints a vivid picture of their lives and preoccupations
in France, *c.* 1405. First English translation.

☐ *La Regenta* **Leopoldo Alas**   £10.95

This first English translation of this Spanish masterpiece has been
acclaimed as 'a major literary event' – *Observer*. 'Among the select
band of "world novels" . . . outstandingly well translated' – John
Bayley in the *Listener*

☐ *Metamorphoses* **Ovid**   £2.95

The whole of Western literature has found inspiration in Ovid's
poem, a golden treasury of myths and legends that are linked by the
theme of transformation.

☐ *Darkness at Noon*   **Arthur Koestler**   £2.50

'Koestler approaches the problem of ends and means, of love and
truth and social organization, through the thoughts of an Old Bolshe-
vik, Rubashov, as he awaits death in a G.P.U. prison' – *New Statesman*

☐ *War and Peace* **Leo Tolstoy**   £4.95

'A complete picture of human life;' wrote one critic, 'a complete
picture of the Russia of that day; a complete picture of everything in
which people place their happiness and greatness, their grief and
humiliation.'

☐ *The Divine Comedy: 1 Hell* **Dante**   £2.25

A new translation by Mark Musa, in which the poet is conducted by
the spirit of Virgil down through the twenty-four closely described
circles of hell.

ENGLISH AND AMERICAN LITERATURE IN PENGUINS

☐ *Emma* **Jane Austen** £1.25

'I am going to take a heroine whom no one but myself will much like,' declared Jane Austen of Emma, her most spirited and controversial heroine in a comedy of self-deceit and self-discovery.

☐ *Tender is the Night* **F. Scott Fitzgerald** £2.95

Fitzgerald worked on seventeen different versions of this novel, and its obsessions – idealism, beauty, dissipation, alcohol and insanity – were those that consumed his own marriage and his life.

☐ *The Life of Johnson* **James Boswell** £2.95

Full of gusto, imagination, conversation and wit, Boswell's immortal portrait of Johnson is as near a novel as a true biography can be, and still regarded by many as the finest 'life' ever written. This shortened version is based on the 1799 edition.

☐ *A House and its Head* **Ivy Compton-Burnett** £4.95

In a novel 'as trim and tidy as a hand-grenade' (as Pamela Hansford Johnson put it), Ivy Compton-Burnett penetrates the facade of a conventional, upper-class Victorian family to uncover a chasm of violent emotions – jealousy, pain, frustration and sexual passion.

☐ *The Trumpet Major* **Thomas Hardy** £1.50

Although a vein of unhappy unrequited love runs through this novel, Hardy also draws on his warmest sense of humour to portray Wessex village life at the time of the Napoleonic wars.

☐ *The Complete Poems of Hugh MacDiarmid*

☐ Volume One £8.95
☐ Volume Two £8.95

The definitive edition of work by the greatest Scottish poet since Robert Burns, edited by his son Michael Grieve, and W. R. Aitken.

ENGLISH AND AMERICAN LITERATURE IN PENGUINS

☐ *Main Street* **Sinclair Lewis** £4.95

The novel that added an immortal chapter to the literature of America's Mid-West, *Main Street* contains the comic essence of Main Streets everywhere.

☐ *The Compleat Angler* **Izaak Walton** £2.50

A celebration of the countryside, and the superiority of those in 1653, as now, who love *quietnesse, vertue* and, above all, *Angling*. 'No fish, however coarse, could wish for a doughtier champion than Izaak Walton' – Lord Home

☐ *The Portrait of a Lady* **Henry James** £2.50

'One of the two most brilliant novels in the language', according to F. R. Leavis, James's masterpiece tells the story of a young American heiress, prey to fortune-hunters but not without a will of her own.

☐ *Hangover Square* **Patrick Hamilton** £3.95

Part love story, part thriller, and set in the publands of London's Earls Court, this novel caught the conversational tone of a whole generation in the uneasy months before the Second World War.

☐ *The Rainbow* **D. H. Lawrence** £2.50

Written between *Sons and Lovers* and *Women in Love*, *The Rainbow* covers three generations of Brangwens, a yeoman family living on the borders of Nottinghamshire.

☐ *Vindication of the Rights of Woman*
   Mary Wollstonecraft £2.95

Although Walpole once called her 'a hyena in petticoats', Mary Wollstonecraft's vision was such that modern feminists continue to go back and debate the arguments so powerfully set down here.

PENGUIN OMNIBUSES

☐ **Victorian Villainies**   £5.95

Fraud, murder, political intrigue and horror are the ingredients of these four Victorian thrillers, selected by Hugh Greene and Graham Greene.

☐ **The Balkan Trilogy** Olivia Manning   £5.95

This acclaimed trilogy – *The Great Fortune, The Spoilt City* and *Friends and Heroes* – is the portrait of a marriage, and an exciting recreation of civilian life in the Second World War. 'It amuses, it diverts, and it informs' – Frederick Raphael

☐ **The Penguin Collected Stories of**
   Isaac Bashevis Singer   £5.95

Forty-seven marvellous tales of Jewish magic, faith and exile. 'Never was the Nobel Prize more deserved . . . He belongs with the giants' – *Sunday Times*

☐ **The Penguin Essays of George Orwell**   £4.95

Famous pieces on 'The Decline of the English Murder', 'Shooting an Elephant', political issues and P. G. Wodehouse feature in this edition of forty-one essays, criticism and sketches – all classics of English prose.

☐ **Further Chronicles of Fairacre** 'Miss Read'   £3.95

Full of humour, warmth and charm, these four novels – *Miss Clare Remembers, Over the Gate, The Fairacre Festival* and *Emily Davis* – make up an unforgettable picture of English village life.

☐ **The Penguin Complete Sherlock Holmes**
   Sir Arthur Conan Doyle   £5.95

With the fifty-six classic short stories, plus *A Study in Scarlet, The Sign of Four, The Hound of the Baskervilles* and *The Valley of Fear*, this volume contains the remarkable career of Baker Street's most famous resident.

PENGUIN OMNIBUSES

☐ *Life with Jeeves* **P. G. Wodehouse** £3.95

Containing *Right Ho, Jeeves, The Inimitable Jeeves* and *Very Good, Jeeves!* in which Wodehouse lures us, once again, into the ever-green world of Bertie Wooster, his terrifying Aunt Agatha, his man Jeeves and other eggs, good and bad.

☐ *The Penguin Book of Ghost Stories* £4.95

An anthology to set the spine tingling, including stories by Zola, Kleist, Sir Walter Scott, M. R. James, Elizabeth Bowen and A. S. Byatt.

☐ *The Penguin Book of Horror Stories* £4.95

Including stories by Maupassant, Poe, Gautier, Conan Doyle, L. P. Hartley and Ray Bradbury, in a selection of the most horrifying horror from the eighteenth century to the present day.

☐ *The Penguin Complete Novels of Jane Austen* £5.95

Containing the seven great novels: *Sense and Sensibility, Pride and Prejudice, Mansfield Park, Emma, Northanger Abbey, Persuasion* and *Lady Susan*.

☐ *Perfick, Perfick!* **H. E. Bates** £4.95

The adventures of the irrepressible Larkin family, in four novels: *The Darling Buds of May, A Breath of French Air, When the Green Woods Laugh* and *Oh! To Be in England*.

☐ *Famous Trials*
   Harry Hodge and James H. Hodge £3.95

From Madeleine Smith to Dr Crippen and Lord Haw-Haw, this volume contains the most sensational murder and treason trials, selected by John Mortimer from the classic Penguin Famous Trials series.